Harwood Fundamentals of Pure and Applied Economics

STABILIZATION AND GROWTH IN DEVELOPING COUNTRIES

FUNDAMENTALS OF PURE AND APPLIED ECONOMICS

DEVELOPMENT ECONOMICS
In 2 Volumes

I	Stabilization and Growth in Developing Countries	*Taylor*
II	Agrarian Structure and Economic Underdevelopment	*Basu*

STABILIZATION AND GROWTH IN DEVELOPING COUNTRIES

A Structuralist Approach

LANCE TAYLOR

ROUTLEDGE
Taylor & Francis Group

First published in 1989 by
Harwood Academic Publishers GmbH

Reprinted in 2001 by
Routledge
2 Park Square, Milton Park, Abingdon, Oxon, OX14 4RN

711 Third Avenue, New York, NY 10017

Transferred to Digital Printing 2007

Routledge is an imprint of the Taylor & Francis Group

First issued in paperback 2013

British Library Cataloguing in Publication Data
A CIP catalogue record for this book
is available from the British Library

ISBN13: 978-0-415-26978-0 (HB Version)

ISBN13: 978-0-415-86611-8 (PB Version)

Stabilization and Growth in Developing Countries A Structuralist Approach

Lance Taylor
Massachusetts Institute of Technology, USA

A volume in the Economic Development Studies section
edited by
S. Chakravarty
Delhi School of Economics, University of Delhi, India

harwood academic publishers
chur · london · paris · new york · melbourne

Harwood Academic Publishers

Post Office Box 197
London WC2E 9PX
England

58, rue Lhomond
75005 Paris
France

Post Office Box 786
Cooper Station
New York, NY 10276
United States of America

Private Bag 8
Camberwell, Victoria 3124
Australia

Library of Congress Cataloging-in-Publication Data

Taylor, Lance.
Stabilization and growth in developing countries: a structuralist approach/Lance Taylor

p. cm.—(Fundamentals of pure and applied economics; v. 29. Economic development studies section)
Bibliography: p.
Includes index.
ISBN 3-7186-4871-7
1. Developing countries—Economic policy. 2. Economic stabilization—Developing countries. 3. Finance—Developing countries. I. Title. II. Series: Fundamentals of pure and applied economics: v. 29. III. Series: Fundamentals of pure and applied economics. Economic development studies section.
HC59.7.T3718 1988
338.9'009172'4—dc19 88-39943
CIP

Contents

Introduction to the Series

Drawing on a personal network, an economist can still relatively easily stay well informed in the narrow field in which he works, but to keep up with the development of economics as a whole is a much more formidable challenge. Economists are confronted with difficulties associated with the rapid development of their discipline. There is a risk of "balkanization" in economics, which may not be favorable to its development.

Fundamentals of Pure and Applied Economics has been created to meet this problem. The discipline of economics has been subdivided into sections (listed inside). These sections include short books, each surveying the state of the art in a given area.

Each book starts with the basic elements and goes as far as the most advanced results. Each should be useful to professors needing material for lectures, to graduate students looking for a global view of a particular subject, to professional economists wishing to keep up with the development of their science, and to researchers seeking convenient information on questions that incidentally appear in their work.

Each book is thus a presentation of the state of the art in a particular field rather than a step-by-step analysis of the development of the literature. Each is a high-level presentation but accessible to anyone with a solid background in economics, whether engaged in business, government, international organizations, teaching, or research in related fields.

Three aspects of *Fundamentals of Pure and Applied Economics* should be emphasized:

—First, the project covers the whole field of economics, not only theoretical or mathematical economics.

—Second, the project is open-ended and the number of books is not predetermined. If new interesting areas appear, they will generate additional books.
—Last, all the books making up each section will later be grouped to constitute one or several volumes of an Encyclopedia of Economics.

The editors of the sections are outstanding economists who have selected as authors for the series some of the finest specialists in the world.

J. Lesourne *H. Sonnenschein*

Stabilization and Growth in Developing Countries: A Structuralist Approach

LANCE TAYLOR

Massachusetts Institute of Technology

A basic model for macro policy analysis is set out, incorporating an inflation theory based on distributional conflict, output and current account adjustment mechanisms, and the money market. Classical structuralist results about contractionary devaluation and stagflationary monetary restriction are derived. Alternative closures of the model are considered—monetarism and external strangulation (or foreign exchange bonanzas)—and it is extended to deal with interest rate reform. Short-term stabilization issues are considered—monetary and fiscal policy, import quotas and export subsidies as opposed to devaluation, financial market complications, food subsidies and public sector pricing, and orthodox and heterodox anti-inflationary programs. Medium-term processes of inflation, distribution, growth, and shifts in the macroeconomic regime are discussed. Finally, how the analysis can be extended to several sectors is briefly sketched.

1. INTRODUCTION

There has been an explosion of work on stabilization and growth problems in developing countries since the late 1970's—the only boon from economic hardship is this outbrust of thought. Before 1980, the consensus among economists trained around the North Atlantic about how to stabilize and grow followed monetarist lines in the short run and neoclassical price-fixing in the long. The center of gravity has shifted toward structuralism since then. This monograph can be read as an attempt to summarize structuralist views as of the mid–1980's, with an emphasis on how practical policy may be designed. A frankly partisan stance regarding the merits of different approaches to developing country macroeconomics is adopted. Orthodox/IMF policies have been amply tested over the past decades in the Third World, and found wanting. Tests of structuralist packages are underway or in the offing. It is high time for concrete policy models to be laid out, if structuralism is to fare better in current practice than mainstream economics has done in the past.

Structuralist analysis is summarized here in a single accounting frame-work or macroeconomic model, extended to deal with specific topics as they arise. The discussion is analytical; except where it is essential, institutional detail has been suppressed. A more institutionally oriented and policy-focused presentation of structuralist ideas appears in Taylor [44].

Three comments should be made about the spirit of the argument. First, algebra is set up in terms of accounting identities observed in all countries, and can easily be recast in numerical terms to give projections of the effects of exogenous changes or policy shifts. All the theoretical results could easily be quantified on a microcomputer.

Second, the model itself can be viewed as a Mundell-Fleming system with explicit treatment of income distribution and inflation dynamics added on. Or, from another angle, it is basically Kalecki's macro scheme, augmented to deal with finance and the external account. Either way, the conclusions are well founded in traditional macroeconomics.

Third, and most important, results are highly dependent on assumptions about the roles of different economic actors, the presence or absence of certain markets, and so on. There is no single macro model for all developing countries. But the argument here is that applicable models can be generated from consistent reasoning based on accounting identities and respect for institutional facts. Many of the problems that made-in-the-North economists create when they come South stem from ignoring these simple precepts.

In what follows, the basic analytical structure is presented in chapter 2, where it is argued that to capture adequately the characteristics of a developing economy open to trade one needs four key relationships—an inflation theory, equations for internal and external balance, and a description of the financial market(s). The details will depend on institutional characteristics of the economy at hand. However, typically there will be an element of cost determination in prices, with components of cost (the wage and exchange rate, principally) responding to past inflation and social conflict. Non-standard effects such as inflation taxes, contractionary devaluation and cost-push from interest rate increases affect macro balance in the Third World, and are spelled out in detail. Financial adjustment under asset indexation is also described.

Chapter 3 develops variations around a theme of macroeconomic causality—directions of effects of policy changes are shown to depend strongly on the "closure" of the system that one adopts. Monetarism is interpreted as a closure in which an assumption of full utilization of capacity is imposed on the internal balance relationship. Reduction of inflation through monetary restraint and wage repression is discussed in this context; on its own assumptions the policy is effective. The operational question is whether the assumptions apply. The same general query is relevant when external balance is constrained—by scarce external resources under "external strangulation" or plentiful ones when there is a dollar bonanza. Macro adjustment difficulties under these two sets of circumstances are considered. Finally, financial market closure is explored in terms of an interest rate reform. Raising deposit rates in an attempt to improve financial performance is shown to be unproductive.

Chapter 4 takes up policy matters that have been at the forefront of discussion the past few years—export subsidies or import quotas (the verdict on their effectiveness is positive), food subsidies and food price inflation (both tricky issues), public enterprise pricing (complex effects), orthodox anti-inflation shocks (generally, they produce bad results) and the heterodox shocks that have recently been attempted in Latin America.

Chapter 5 is a review of factors affecting income distribution and growth in the long run. The key adjusting variables are the real wage and real exchange rate, and their dynamics is considered under various closures. Regime shifts between adjustment and forced saving/inflation tax adjustment are next taken up. The chapter closes with a sketch of how its results can be extended to deal with multiple sectors and economic classes.

Finally, a word should be added about how the models set out here relate to other literature. The structuralist tradition in macroeconomics is an old one—Kindleberger [23] traces it back at least 300 years. Its latest flowering near the North Atlantic was stimulated by Kalecki and Keynes. A Latin American school which explicitly adopted the structuralist label took off soon after, partly in response to their work.

Arndt's [2a] capsule history traces lineages between North Atlantic and Latin thought. Similar ideas flourished in India and the Caribbean which Arndt does not discuss. The main themes in all this literature are that institutions and available technology strongly constrain change in an economy at any point in time. In particular, these limitations (unless changed consciously by political action and economic policy or unconsciously by historical forces) may rule out a rapid, equitable development path. Unfavorable outcomes could include inflation based on distributional conflict provoked by lagging agricultural supply as discussed by Noyola Vasquez [33], external imbalances of the type later formalized in the two-gap model of Chenery and Bruno [9], and adverse trends in the terms of trade for countries exporting primary products in an increasingly unfavourable world market.

The analysis here draws upon all developing economy structuralists as well as the economists (Robinson, Kaldor, and disciples) at the University of Cambridge who followed Keynes. Over the past 20 years, a "neostructuralist" school has appeared. For short run stabilization problems, its work emphasizes that developing economies may respond to standard policies in unexpected ways—devaluation may cause output contraction, tight money may lead to price increases due to higher interest costs, inflation is likely to have its own "inertial" dynamics, public investment may crowd private capital formation in instead of out. Stabilization programs are unlikely to succeed if their constituent policies are not designed taking such responses into account.

In the longer run, the recent authors emphasize the importance of the income distribution in conditioning the growth process. Like their predecessors, they tend to be sceptical about the benefits of market liberalization and unfettered external capital flows and trade. They often propose models of unstable macroeconomic dynamic processes that liberalization can provoke.

This monograph pulls together many of the neostructuralists's ideas, including the examples just pointed out. The younger authors have gone much further than their predecessors in formalizing and tracing through the logical implications of the macro adjustment processes they invoke. The models herein elaborate the tricks developed by these economists in their trade, but leave out the historical and institutional richness of their way of looking at the world. For that, the reader will have to turn to their cited work.

2. THE BASIC MODEL

The modelling strategy follows Kalecki [21] in dealing with wage and profit recipients (or "workers" and "capitalists") and the state as the main economic actors. Extensions toward agricultural and non-agricultural groups as well as the ubiquitous "foreigners" on the other side of the balance of payments are brought in from time to time. This class analysis is rudimentary, but has the advantage of fitting with available functional income distribution data. It can and should be extended in specific country contexts, especially since behavioral differences across classes (and conflicts among them) are key explanatory factors for much macroeconomics in the Third World.

For simpler mathematics, we work with continuous time, even though in concrete numerical simulation, discrete time periods (a quarter or a year) make more sense. Stability analysis refers either to a "short run" (a quarter or so) during which output levels and some prices can change, or to a "long run" as conventionally represented by growth in a steady state. By and large, we work with only one producing sector and keep asset and liability categories to a feasible minimum. Financial dealings largely take place between the "public" or "capitalists" and firms, unrealistically omitting transactions among the latter. Asset markets are assumed to clear by changes in prices or interest rates, even though quantity clearing under controls is characteristic in the Third World. Analytical ease is the justification, with the caveat that interest rate increases in a model can always be read as "credit tightness" in real markets.

There are four basic macro equations and corresponding accounts—the decomposition of the unit price of output into costs, the balance between output and sources of demand, balances between demands and supplies of financial assets (with an emphasis on money), and the external payments accounts. Flows-of-funds further link excesses (or shortfalls) of savings over investment flows from the real side of the economy to accumulation of assets (or liabilities) in its financial sphere.

2.1. Price formation and inflation rates

Firms' costs decompose into purchases of intermediate inputs (both imported and nationally produced), the wage bill, profits and paid-out earnings, and interest charges. Since we are working with one sector, national intermediate costs can in principle be reduced to primary and imported inputs through the input-output system, and we further assume that some interest payments can be traced to the finance of working capital. Production is supposed to take place under "industrial" and/or oligopolistic conditions, so that mark-up pricing along the lines urged by Kalecki [21] and Sylos-Labini [38] is a plausible behavior rule. The mark-up is defined over prime cost of labor and imported intermediates. Prime cost per unit of output, or B, is

$$B = wb + eP_0^*a \tag{1}$$

where w is the money wage, b the labor-output ratio, e the nominal exchange rate P_0^* the price of imported intermediate inputs in the world markets, and a the input-output coefficient for intermediates.

Let ω be the period over which prime inputs must be financed as working capital, i the nominal rate of interest on loans to firms, τ the mark-up rate over interest-inclusive prime costs, and v the rate of indirect taxation on final goods' prices. Then the overall price level P will be given by the equation

$$P = (1 + v)(1 + \tau)(1 + i\omega)B \tag{2}$$

Note that in an "instantaneous" period, an increase in the interest rate, exchange rate, tax rate, wage rate or mark-up rate will drive up the price level from (1) and (2). The positive impact of interest rates on prices via costs goes under various labels—it is called the "Wright Patman effect" after the late easy-money Congressman from Texas by Americans, and attributed to Cavallo [7] in Latin lands. Like many "effects" in macroeconomics, it has been observed, forgotten, and rediscovered over the years. References from a generation ago included Streeten and Balogh [37] and Galbraith [16]. The positive influences on prices of the other components of cost are all widely recognized, although as we will see in Section 4.1, the price-increasing impact of nominal devaluation (an increase in e) in the presence of trade quotas is occasionally denied.

In practice, changes in most components of cost do not occur in an instant, but rather are spread over time. In an inflationary environment like that in many developing countries, it is reasonable to assume that firms stay on or near their desired cost schedules. Hence, equations like (1) and (2) will hold in growth rate form as well. If we let a circumflex accent or "hat" over a variable denote its rate of growth, price inflation $\hat{P}$ from (1) and (2) can be decomposed in terms of variables that evolve over time as

$$\hat{P} = \frac{\tau}{1+\tau}\hat{\tau} + (1-\phi)\hat{w} + \phi\hat{e} \tag{3}$$

where $\phi = eP_0^*a/B$ is the share of imported intermediates in prime costs.

As (3) makes clear, we are treating the tax rate v, interest rate i, etc., in (1) and (2) as "jump" variables that affect the price *level* but not its growth rate $\hat{P}$. The exchange rate e can either jump in what the Brazilians in an era of unstable skirt lengths called a maxi-devaluation or grow steadily at rate $\hat{e}$ in a sequence of mini-devaluations or a crawling peg.

Decisions of firm-owners and workers jointly determine how mark-up and wage rates change. If we measure activity by the output-capital ratio u, then mark-up dynamics in the time-frame of (3) can be written as

$$\hat{\tau} = \alpha(u - \bar{u}_\tau). \tag{4}$$

The parameter α plays a central role in the discussion that follows. The stylized fact, mostly based on evidence from industrialized countries, is that the real wage varies positively with the level of activity, i.e. the mark-up rate falls when u rises or $\alpha < 0$. However, monetarist macro models often invoke a hidden assumption that $\alpha > 0$, so that more profit income goes hand-in-hand with economic expansion. As argued here and in Taylor [41], the qualitative nature of macro adjustment depends strongly on the sign of α. Unsurprisingly, an economist's prior assumptions about α are a good indication of her world-view.

Let $z = w/P$ be the real wage. We assume that workers press for increases in the money wage—the nominal price over which they have some control—when the real wage is low and/or the level of economic activity high:

$$\hat{w} = \psi(u - \bar{u}_w) - \lambda(z - \bar{z}). \tag{5}$$

Distributed lags could well embellish both terms on the right. In practice, an extended wage equation of the form $\hat{w} = \kappa\hat{P} + \phi(u - \bar{u}_w) - \lambda(z - \bar{z})$ may apply, where κ is a "pass-through coefficient" of price inflation into wages. Pass-through matters little in theory, but can be vital in practice. As illustrated in Section 3.1, orthodox inflation stabilization often is built around reductions in social parameters like κ.

Solving these equations gives a reduced form for price inflation as

$$\begin{aligned}\hat{P} &= \frac{\tau\alpha}{1-\tau}(u - \bar{u}_\tau) + (1-\phi)\psi(u - \bar{u}_w) - (1-\phi)\lambda(z - \bar{z}) + \phi\hat{e} \\ &= \hat{P}_0 + \left[\frac{\tau\alpha}{1+\tau} + (1-\phi)\right]u - (1-\phi)\lambda z + \phi\hat{e} \qquad (6)\end{aligned}$$

where $\hat{P}_0$ is a constant term. The coefficient on u in second line can in principle take either sign, but is likely to be positive. Its magnitude will be small compared to the cost terms when inflation is self-perpetuating or "inertial" as discussed in Section 4.5. The reduced form for the growth rate of the real wage ($\hat{z} = \hat{w} - \hat{P}$) is

$$\begin{aligned}\hat{z} &= -\frac{\tau\alpha}{1+\tau}(u - \bar{u}_\tau) + \phi\psi(u - \bar{u}_w) - \phi\lambda(z - \bar{z}) - \phi\hat{e} \\ &= \hat{z}_0 + \left[\phi\psi - \frac{\tau\alpha}{1+\tau}\right]u - \phi\lambda z - \phi e \qquad (7)\end{aligned}$$

where $\hat{z}_0$ is another intercept term.

These equations can generate complex distributional dynamics. If the rate of exchange depreciation $\hat{e}$ is predetermined, (4) and (7) are independent relationships. In long-run steady state, (4) shows that capacity utilization must be at a level $\bar{u}_\tau$ to hold the mark-up constant. The real wage, meanwhile, will be a decreasing function of $\hat{e}$ when $\hat{z} = 0$ at steady state from (7). If a purely accommodative crawling peg is pursued, with $\hat{e}$ always set equal to $\hat{P}$, then (4) and (7) reduce to same equation with $\hat{\tau} = \hat{z} = 0$ at a steady state with $u = \bar{u}_\tau$. In either case, since we are ignoring productivity change, all nominal prices will have the same inflation rate, $\hat{P} = \hat{w} = \hat{e}$, under steady state conditions. Long run implications for distribution and growth of these different inflation patterns are discussed in chapter 5.

2.2. Internal and external balance

The decomposition of production costs underlying the foregoing price equations takes the form

$$PX = wbX + eP_0^*ax + \tau(1+i\omega)BX + i\omega BX + v(1+\tau)(1+i\omega)BX \quad (8)$$

where X is the real output. This equation shows that the value of output is equal to the sum of the wage bill, intermediate import costs, mark-up income, interest on working capital, and value-added taxes. The output concept is larger than GDP, since it includes non-competitive intermediate imports.

The corresponding decomposition on the demand side is

$$PX = PC + P\theta I + PE + PG, \quad (9)$$

where the symbols have the usual meanings, except that θ is the share of gross investment produced nationally (the balance is imported) and E should be interpreted as exports net of competitive imports.

The next step is to set out behavioral rules for the terms on the right side of (9). The consumption function (again ignoring lags) can be written as

$$PC = PC_0(\hat{P}) + wbX + (1-s)[\tau(1+i\omega)BX + i\omega BX] \quad (10)$$

in which it is assumed that the marginal propensities to consume from wage and non-wage incomes are unity and $(1-s)$ respectively. The intercept term $C_0(\hat{P})$ is assumed to depend on the inflation rate, with uncertain sign. If real balance effects or inflation taxes are important (Section 3.1), the derivative of C_0 would be negative. If inflation reduction frightens (or bankrupts) previously high-spending debtors, then lower consumption might follow, giving $dC_0/d\hat{P}$ a positive sign. A practically more important effect is likely to be fiscal drag from a less than fully indexed tax collection system. Slower inflation under such circumstances reduces the fiscal deficit, giving a positive relationship between $\hat{P}$ and aggregate demand.

En route to an investment function, recall that we have defined capacity utilization or the output-capital ratio as $u = X/K$, where K is the capital stock. Since capital in place is made up of nationally produced and imported components (think of plant and equipment) in proportions θ and $1-\theta$, its price P_k will be given by $P_k = \theta P + (1-\theta)eP_i^*$, where P_i^* is the world price of imported capital goods. Total profits are $\tau(1+i\omega)BX$, and the profit rate is

$$r = \frac{\tau(1+i\omega)BX}{P_k K} = \frac{\tau}{(1+v)(1+\tau)[\theta + (1-\theta)qP_i^*]} u.$$

This expression shows that the profit rate is proportional (through a hideous coefficient) to capacity utilization. In the denominator of the final term, we introduce $q = e/P$, or the real exchange rate. More compactly, we can call the coefficient β and write the profit rate as

$$r = \beta(v, \tau, q)u \tag{11}$$

in which partial derivatives of β with respect to all terms are negative, except that $\partial\beta/\partial\tau > 0$.

We will assume that most investment is financed by borrowing from banks or the public. Investment demand should respond positively to the profit rate as an index of expected future gain, and negatively to the real interest rate $i - \hat{P}$, where i is the nominal rate on loans taken by firms. A direct effect of the mark-up rate on investment demand is also possible, as suggested by Marglin and Bhaduri [28]. The overall investment function becomes

$$\begin{aligned} I &= [g_0(\tau) + h(r - (i - \hat{P}))]K \\ &= [g_0(\tau) + h\beta(v, \tau, q)u - h(i - \hat{P})]K \end{aligned} \tag{12}$$

where the second line follows by substitution from (11).

The remaining components of final demand are government spending G, assumed to be a policy variable, and net exports E. The volume of exports can be assumed to respond to "our" prices as seen abroad, $P(1-\zeta)/e$, where ζ is a rate of export subsidy, and the price of foreign similars, P_e^*. A formal expression is

$$E = E\left[\frac{eP_e^*}{P(1-\zeta)}\right] \tag{13}$$

with a positive slope.

Elimination of terms between (8) and (9) gives the condition that excess demand for commodities should equal zero, or an investment-saving balance of the form

$$\begin{aligned} &[P\theta + eP_i^*(1-\theta)]I + [PG + \zeta PE - v(1+\tau)(1+i\omega)BX] \\ &\qquad + eT - \{s[\tau(1+i\omega) + i\omega]BX - PC_0(\hat{P})\} = 0 \end{aligned} \tag{14}$$

in which gross capital formation, the government deficit (government purchases plus export susidies less taxes), and the trade surplus (eT) are financed by saving from profits less than consumption intercept $PC_0(\hat{P})$. The trade balance is

$$(1-\zeta)PE - eP_0^*aX - eP_i^*(1-\theta)I - eT = 0. \tag{15}$$

Equations (14) and (15) appear in the literature under various names, as discussed in Bacha [3] and Taylor [40]. The former is known as an internal balance relationship, or the saving gap. Equation (14) defines external balance, or the trade gap. We will find it useful to normalize these expressions by the capital stock (or, in numerical models, one might use potential output). Dividing (14) by PK and some rearrangement of terms give

$$c_0(\hat{P}) + (\theta + q(1-\theta)P_i^*)[g_0(\tau) - h(i-\hat{P})] + \left[\frac{(h-s)\tau}{(1+v)(1+\tau)} - \frac{v}{1+v} - \frac{si\omega}{(1+v)(1+\tau)(1+i\omega)}\right]u + \gamma + \zeta\varepsilon[q, P_e^*, (1-\zeta)] + qt = 0 \tag{16}$$

in which $c_0 = C_0/K$, $q = e/P$, $u = X/K$, $\gamma = G/K$, $\varepsilon = E/K$, and $t = T/K$, and we also define the growth rate of capital stock as $g = I/K$.

The corresponding equation for the trade surplus is

$$\frac{(1-\zeta)\varepsilon(q, P_e^*, 1-\zeta)}{q} - P_0^*au - (1-\theta)P_i^*[g_0(\tau) + h\beta(v, \tau, \theta)u - h(i-\hat{P})] - t = 0 \tag{17}$$

Occasionally we will find it useful to work with aggregate demand directly, consolidating interactions between u and t. The corresponding balance equation follows from substitution of (17) into (16), and is

$$c_0(\hat{P}) + \gamma + \varepsilon + \theta[g_0(\tau) - h(i-\hat{P})] + \left[\frac{\tau}{(1+v)(1+s)}\left(\frac{h\theta}{\theta + (1-\theta)aP_i^*} - s\right) - \frac{v}{1+v} - \frac{si\omega + \phi}{(1+v)(1+\tau)(1+i\omega)}\right]u = 0, \tag{18}$$

where $\phi = eP_0^*a/(wb + eP_0^*a)$. In (18) as opposed to (16), total exports ε enter as a component of final demand, and intermediate import costs ϕ are a saving leakage proportional to capacity utilization u.

2.3. The trade surplus and acitvity level

Equations (16) and (17) are two relationships among four adjusting variables in the short run—capacity utilization u, the trade surplus t, the interest rate i, and inflation $\hat{P}$. We have already set up (6) as a cost-and-activity-based explanation of the inflation rate, and will shortly derive an equation from the financial market for the interest rate. The outcome is a 4×4 system, which it will be convenient to solve by eliminating $\hat{P}$ and i and working in a diagram for u and t. Preparatory to that, it makes sense to run through the direct interactions of capacity utilization and the trade surplus with the rest of the system. The relevant derivatives appear formally in Eq. (A.1) in the appendix. From the algebra, we can observe the following points:

First, in the bracketed term multiplying u in (16), the usual short run stability condition is $h < s$, or the accelerator effect of a higher profit rate on investment demand is less than the extra saving generated. Since the other terms in the bracket are negative tax and saving leakages, it is easy to see that a higher trade balance t raises the level of economic activity (other things being equal). Increased net exports bid up demand for available resources over saving in (14) or (16), and output in consequence rises. By contrast, extra activity requires more intermediate imports in (15) or (17) and causes the trade surplus to fall. These cross linkages between internal and external balance carrying over when feedbacks from i and $\hat{P}$ are taken into account, as shown in Figure 1 below.

Second, faster inflation increases investment demand by reducing the real interest rate (the "Tobin effect"). At the same time, it may either stimulate or frustrate consumption as discussed above. Hence, inflation's effect on capacity utilization is ambiguous, but by increasing investment it causes the trade surplus to fall. A higher nominal interest rate has no consumption effect, but by reducing investment makes u fall and t rise.

Third, a higher tax rate or reduced government spending cuts back on activity. Neither has a direct effect on the trade surplus.

Fourth, an increase in the mark-up rate directly stimulates investment demand. On the other hand, it reduces the average propensity to consume, leading to contraction (the second term in the first line of the vector multiplying $d\tau$ in equation (A.1)). The overall effect on aggregate demand of this sort of redistribution is ambiguous, as noted by Dutt [12] and discussed more fully in section 5.1. By contrast, an increase in τ worsens the trade balance by increasing capital goods imports.

Fifth, real devaluation (an increase in q) has an ambiguous direct effect on the level of activity. From the first row of the vector multplying dq in (A.1), the sign depends on $(\varepsilon/q) - P_0^*au = (1-\theta)P_i^*g + t$, if the subsidy rate ζ is initially set to zero. There will be added aggregate demand if real exports exceed intermediate imports. From (15), an equivalent condition is that capital goods imports exceed the trade deficit (or physical capital flows from abroad are greater than financial capital inflows plus transfers). Data on trading patterns of developing countries presented by McCarthy, Taylor, and Talati [29] suggest that the latter condition is often *not* satisfied, so real devaluation may reduce demand. Its effect on the trade surplus is positive (which in turn stimulates demand), so the overall impact on activity is unclear. Using (A.1), it is easy to see that the condition for output expansion in the 2×2 system is $\varepsilon_q > P_0^*au$, where ε_q is the derivative of ε with respect to q. Equivalently, the elasticity of ε must exceed the intermediate import/export ratio for devaluation to be expansionary. Either way, exports have to be fairly responsive to real depreciation if higher capacity utilization is to follow. A weak response makes devaluation contractionary in the short run, a possibility noted by structrualists such as Hirschman [19] and Diaz-Alejandro [10] long ago.

Sixth, the real exchange rate q and wage z depend on other variables in the system. The derivatives appear in equations (A.2) and (A.3) in the appendix. Note that real devaluation will be less than proportional to a nominal exchange rate increase insofar as intermediate imports are a component of prime cost.

Finally, with the real interest rate held constant, investment demand goes up with the level of activity in (12). An expansionary factor in the system (a high trade surplus, for example) leads not only to high capacity utilization but to fast growth.

2.4. Financial markets

In an initial treatment of financial markets, we assume that the private sector (firms and the wealth-holding "public") have no assets or liabilities abroad. Such a financial structure fit many developing countries better in the 1970's than it does today, after their accumulation of private external debt burdens and "dollarization" or domestic finance. Nevertheless, it provides a useful starting point, which is extended to incorporate foreign assets in Section 4.4.

Sample balance sheets appear in Table 1. The government *is* assumed to borrow from foreigners, as well as the central bank. The instrument of monetary control is a credit multiplier (manipulated through reserve requirements, etc.) so that deposits are related to high-powered money by the rule,

$$D = \mu H$$

where μ is the multiplier. Other monetary tools such as rediscount, credit controls, or open market operations could easily be incorporated.

TABLE I
Balance sheets omitting external assets and liabilities of the private sector

	Government		
		eF^*	External Debt
		F	Domestic Debt
	Central Bank		
Loans to government	F	H	High-powered money
Foreign reserves	eR^*		
	Commercial Banks		
Deposit reserves	H	D	Deposits
Loans to firms	L_b		
	Firms		
Capital stock	$P_k K$	L_b	Loans from banks
		L_p	Loans from public
	Public		
Deposit	D	W	Wealth
Loans to firms	L_p		

In an inflationary situation, deposits will bear a rate of return roughly indexed to the inflation rate $\hat{P}$. Demand for deposits therefore *rises* with the inflation rate—in an indexed financial system traditional tales about inflation taxes do not apply (see Section 3.1). Deposit demand will respond negatively to the rate of interest on loans, and it makes sense to assume that it depends positively on the level of activity. Wealth is pre-determined at any time. From the accounting in Table 1, it is the sum of primary assets in the system,

$$W = F + eR^* + P_k K. \tag{19}$$

The interest rate emerges from the equilibrium condition for deposits,

$$\delta(i, \hat{P}, u)(F + eR^* + P_k K) - \mu(F + eR^*) = 0,$$

with $\hat{P}$ and u coming from the non-financial side of the economy. With deposit equilibrium satisfied, it is easy to see from Table 1 that the loan market will clear.

As with the expressions for external and internal balance, it is convenient to restate the deposit equation in ratio form, this time scaled by the state's outstanding liabilities held within the country, F. Define V as the "velocity" of F with respect to the capital stock $P_k K$: $V = P_k K/F$. Velocity here is a state variable, i.e., it is constant in the short run (in line with orthodox views) but evolves over time in response to the inflation rate of capital goods prices, the growth rate of capital, and the expansion of state debt (from the fiscal deficit). Higher velocity corresponds to reduced financial intermediation (again orthodox) but such a situation is the outcome of a combination of factors. The differential equation describing the growth of V is usually stable [41] so it does not fluctuate strongly over time. Nonetheless, since velocity *is* a state variable, simple stories about its constancy or variations cannot apply. The same observations apply to the reserve to debt ratio $\rho : \rho = R^*/F$.

The scaled version of the deposit demand equation is

$$\delta(i, \hat{P}, u)(V + e\rho + 1) - \mu(1 + e\rho) = 0 \tag{20}$$

Contractionary monetary policy (a lower μ) or higher velocity will force δ to fall via a higher interest rate i—no surprises. Faster inflation increases deposit demand according to the partial derivative $\delta_{\hat{P}}$. Since the interest rate derivative δ_i is negative, i will rise to compensate for an increase in $\hat{P}$ and hold δ constant. The own-rate of return should affect deposit demand more than a cross rate, or $\delta_{\hat{P}} > -\delta_i$. The implication is that along the deposit demand schedule, $di/d\hat{P} > 1$. In an indexed financial market, faster inflation *increases* the real rate of interest, $i - \hat{P}$, and thus may cause aggregate demand to decline. Finally, lower activity u in the normal case of asset "crowding-out" will lead deposit demand and therefore the interest rate to fall, although when there is a financial panic and flight toward liquidity the opposite may occur [47].

2.5. Public sector flows of funds

As discussed in connection with (16) and (17), those two equations together with (6) for inflation and (20) for the interest rate comprise a 4×4 system in u, t, $\hat{P}$, and i. Beyond the short run, the real wage will change in (7) and the mark-up rate in (4), physical capital will be accumulated at the rate $g = I/K$, and velocity will change according to the growth equation $\hat{V} = \hat{P}_k + g - \hat{F}$. In this section, we take up the determination of growth in the government's two liability items, domestic and foreign debt F and F^*.

The relevant accounting equations are the government budget identity and the balance of payments. The former is

$$[PG + \zeta PE - v(1+\tau)(1+i\omega)BX] + iF + i^*eF^* = \dot{F} + e\dot{F}^*, \quad (21)$$

where i^* is the interest rate on external debt and a dot above a variable denotes its time increment ($\dot{F} = dF/dt$, etc.). The balance of payments is

$$e\dot{R}^* = eT + e\dot{F} - i^*eF^*. \quad (22)$$

Note that we can remove the foreign debt terms in (21) by substitution from (22). One can divide the resulting expression by F to get the growth rate of domestic government debt as

$$\hat{F} = \frac{1}{1+e\rho}\left[\frac{V}{(\theta + q(1-\theta)P_i^*)}\left(\gamma + \zeta\varepsilon - \frac{v}{1+v}u + qt\right) + i - e\rho\hat{\rho}\right] \quad (23)$$

(terms in $\hat{R}^*$ are eliminated through the identity $\hat{\rho} = \hat{R}^* - \hat{F}$). In (23), a higher trade surplus forces increased domestic borrowing, since the amount of foreign debt that can be brought in through net imports is reduced. Such accounting is painful in economies constrained by foreign resources, as we will see in Section 3.2.

A second unfortunate observation about (23) is that the famous "public sector borrowing requirement" or PSBR (as scaled by the capital stock and the internally held national debt) is

$$PSBR = \frac{V}{\theta + q(1-\theta)P_i^*}\left(\gamma + \zeta\varepsilon - \frac{v}{1+v}\right)u + i$$

which rises with the interest rate i. Under inflation, nominal fiscal spending to pay interest on public debt may be high when i is large, at the same time as the fiscal demand injection term $\gamma + \zeta\varepsilon - uv/(1+v)$ is small. In its stand-by programs the IMF often insists on a low PSBR (as a percent of GNP, say) which means that when i is high, fiscal policy may be strongly contractionary. The effect is worse when, as is frequently the case, the people who design orthodox stabilizations underestimate $\hat{P}$ and i. They preset the PSBR in nominal terms, so that when inflation and interest rates come out higher than predicted, real spending has to be cut to fit the target *ex post*. The pattern repeats itself across programs; one wonders if only forecasting mistakes are involved.

Turning to the foreign accounts, let f be the ratio of foreign to domestic debt, $f = F^*/F$. From (22) its growth rate is

$$\hat{f} = \frac{1}{ef}\left[e(\rho - f)\hat{F} + e\rho\hat{\rho} - \frac{qtV}{\theta + q(1-\theta)P_i^*}\right] + i^* \qquad (24)$$

As in (23), the growth rate of the reserve/debt ratio ρ enters as a policy variable in (24). Faster reserve accumulation requires faster growth in foreign debt, other things being equal. The term $e(\rho - f)\hat{F}$ in (24) reflects the fact that ρ and f are ratio variables—to hold f constant, F^* has to expand at the same rate as F.

2.6. Classic structuralist results in the short run

After all this accounting, we can finally begin to talk about economics. A good place to start is with the observation that equations (16), (17), and (20) are partly decomposable. The activity level and trade surplus interact in (16) and (17), affected by inflation and the interest rate. However, the trade balance does not influence the latter two variables directly, and the effect of i on $\hat{P}$ depends on Cavallo/Patman linkages which may be strong or weak (a higher interest rate makes the price level jump up in (2), reducing the real wage and accelerating inflation in (6)).

Equation (A.5) in the appendix shows interactions of the inflation and interest rates. Inflation depends on distributional variables and the level of activity, while the interest rate is determined by asset choice. To illustrate these different channels, we can consider what happens when there is a nominal devaluation. The rise in the exchange rate increases the local currency value of international reserves leading the supply of bank credit to rise and the interest rate to fall (unless, as often occurs, the devaluation is sterilized in an exchange account in the Central Bank). On the other hand, the real wage declines as the price level jumps with devaluation, leading to more inflation and (through financial markets) higher nominal interest rates. The upshot is that inflation goes up, but the sign of the interest rate change is ambiguous. On the general principle that inflation and interest rates move together, we will assume that i rises along with $\hat{P}$ when there is devaluation. Both also rise in response to increases in the mark-up and indirect tax rates, or to decreases in the money wage. Monetary expansion makes both rates fall.

Having solved for i and $\hat{P}$ from (A.5), it is simple in principle (but messy in practice) to plug the results back into (A.1) to get the reduced form equations mentioned in Section 2.3 for u and t. Feedbacks from inflation and interest rates do not change the slopes described there. As shown in the upper diagram of Figure 1, a higher trade surplus requires a higher activity level to maintain internal balance, while greater activity draws in imports and leads the surplus to decline in the external accounts. The lower diagrams show that both interest and inflation rates rise with capacity utilization (the positions and slopes of the curves of course depend on parameters and predetermined variables).

Figure 1 can be used to illustrate well-known results in the literature on structuralist macroeconomics. First, consider tighter monetary policy (a lower credit multiplier μ or reserve ratio ρ, or an increase in velocity V due to a fall in the government's domestic debt F). From (20) the interest rate rises, reducing investment

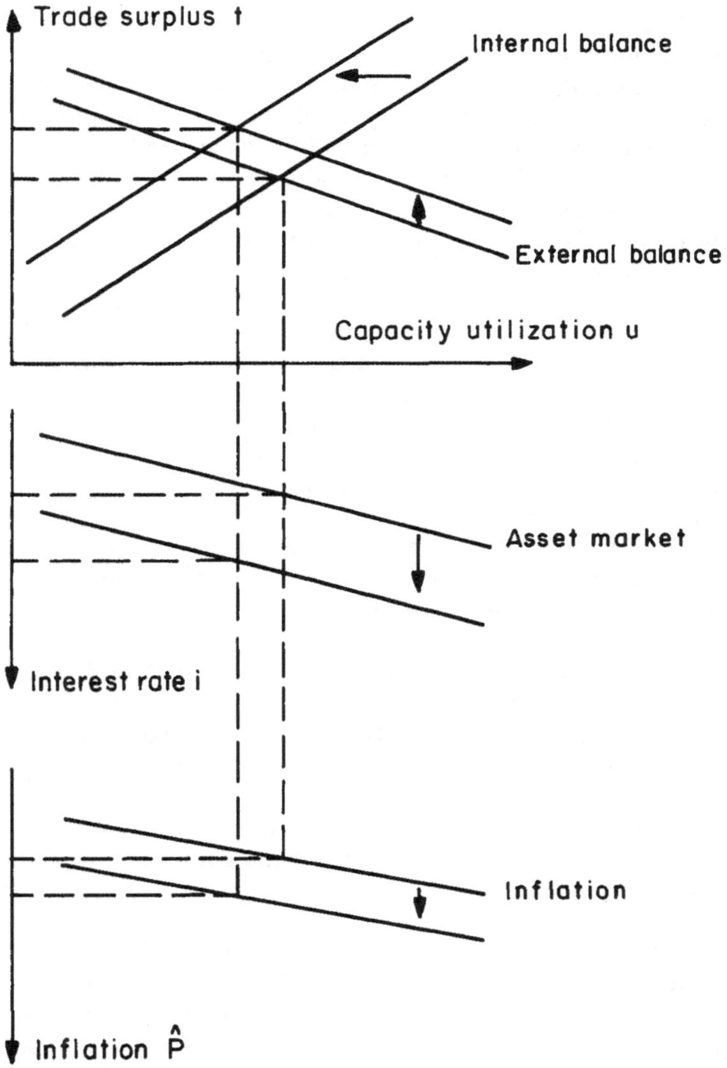

FIGURE 1 The short-run macro system. Monetary contraction leads to reduced activity and a higher trade surplus by increasing the interest rate and reducing investment demand. Inflation immediately accelerates due to a jump in the price level and a lower real wage. It may gradually drop off as the inflation schedule drifts back toward its initial position as the mark-up rate declines in response to lower output.

demand. The internal balance locus shifts to the left, while external balance improves due to reduced capital goods imports. The asset market locus shifts downward as shown, leading to a higher interest rate even at the reduced activity level. From (2) the price level jumps due to cost-push of working capital finance, reducing the real wage and leading to inflationary pressure in (6)—the inflation locus shifts downward. In Figure 1, the shift is shown large enough to create faster inflation at a lower activity level, i.e., contractionary monetary policy is stagflationary. Such an outcome is less likely insofar as α in (4) is strongly positive, so that the mark-up rate declines sharply in response to reduced activity (the inflation locus in Figure 1 has a steep slope). On the other hand, if firms seek to protect cash flow by maintaining or increasing mark-ups when activity slackens ($\alpha < 0$ in (4)), then Cavallo/Wright Patman problems may arise. We will see in Section 3.1 that assuming a strongly positive α to avoid inflationary outcomes from tight money is a characteristic monetarist ploy.

The overall conclusions are that monetary tightness is contractionary and possibly inflationary in the short run, but improves the trade surplus. What can be said about devaluation?

To work out the effects of exchange rate changes in the full model, we have to consider the nominal, not the real, exchange rate since the latter is an endogenous variable (with its responses to the rest of the system given in (A.2)). As discussed above, we assume that a jump in the nominal rate e raises inflation by reducing the real wage through the price level from (1) and (2). By increasing demand for indexed deposits, higher inflation also bids up the nominal interest rate, reducing investment demand. Especially if consumption responds negatively to inflation. (strong real balance or distribution effects), there will be added contraction from devaluation beyond the trade responses discussed in Section 2.3. The outcome would be a leftward shift of the internal balance locus, as in Figure 1. We arrive at the situation similar to that depicted in the figure, where devaluation (like monetary contraction) is stagflationary but trade gap-reducing in the short run.

Following the argument in Section 2.3, devaluation will be expansionary when export response is strong (so the upward shift of the external balance locus in Figure 1 is large) and/or exports initially exceed intermediate imports (in which case the internal balance line would shift rightward instead of leftward). Since both the interest and inflation rates respond to the level of activity, their increases will be sharper when devaluation causes the level of activity to go up.

Whether devaluation is expansionary or contractionary has obvious implications for policy. Using a standard trick to illustrate trade-offs among instruments, Figure 2 provides an illustration. In both diagrams, the $t = \bar{t}$ locus represents a constant trade surplus. Since the surplus rises with both the exchange rate and interest rate, the two policy variables trade off inversely in holding t constant. If devaluation is expansionary, capacity utilization rises with e while it declines with i. To hold $u = \bar{u}$, higher interest rates must be accompanied by devaluation (upper diagram). By contrast, contractionary devaluation leads to a negative e vs. i trade-off, as in the lower graph.

An improvement in the trade balance requires either e or i to rise, as shown by the shifted curves. The implications from solving the model is that trade improvement relies on devaluation, but should be accompanied by easy money when contraction results (lower diagram). In the contractionary case, policy "overkill" can easily result from over-zealous attempts to combine devaluation with tight money as in many IMF packages. Similar reasoning can be applied to inflation/output relationships when a higher interest rate can either slow inflation by reducing excess demand or lead it to accelerate via working capital cost-push. An attempt to reduce demand by tight money leads to faster price increases in the latter case. Fiscal contraction has to be added to higher rates to restrain prices, leading to further output cuts.

These trade-offs are made more difficult to manage by changes in variables over time. For example, the export response to real depreciation will be lagged, which raises dynamic problems. In a concrete illustration, assume that the mark-up rate stays constant, (or α equals zero in (4)). The real exchange rate q will then follow dynamics given by

$$\hat{q} = -\frac{1-\phi}{\phi}\hat{z}$$

where $\hat{z}$ comes from (7). One can just as well assume that exports depend on the real wage as the exchange rate in a formulation

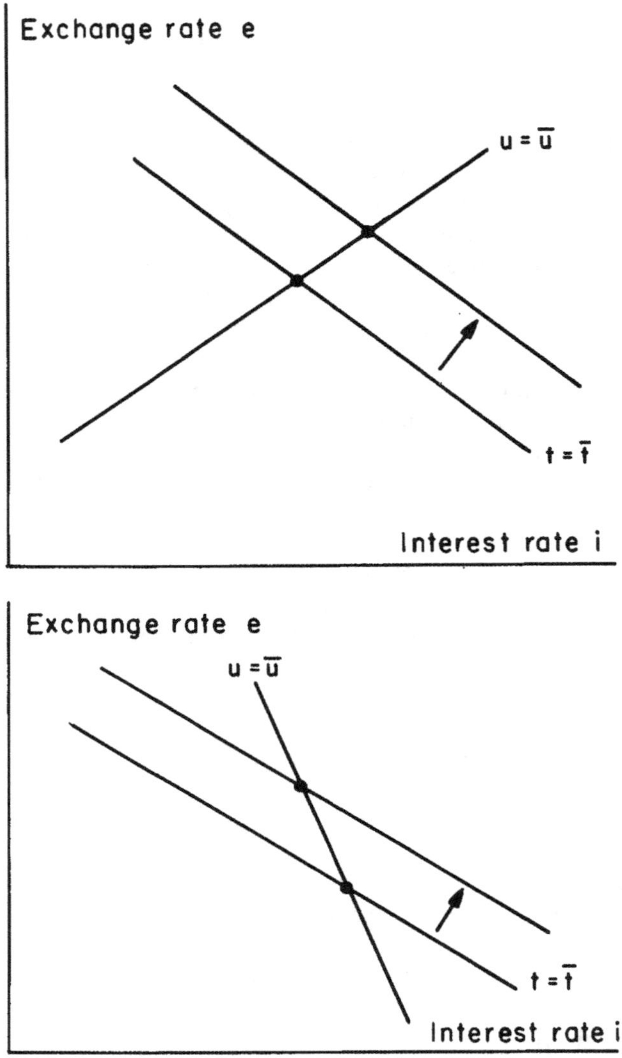

FIGURE 2 Changes in the exchange rate and interest rate required to increase the trade surplus while the level of activity is held steady. The upper and lower diagrams illustrate situations in which devaluation is expansionary and contractionary, respectively.

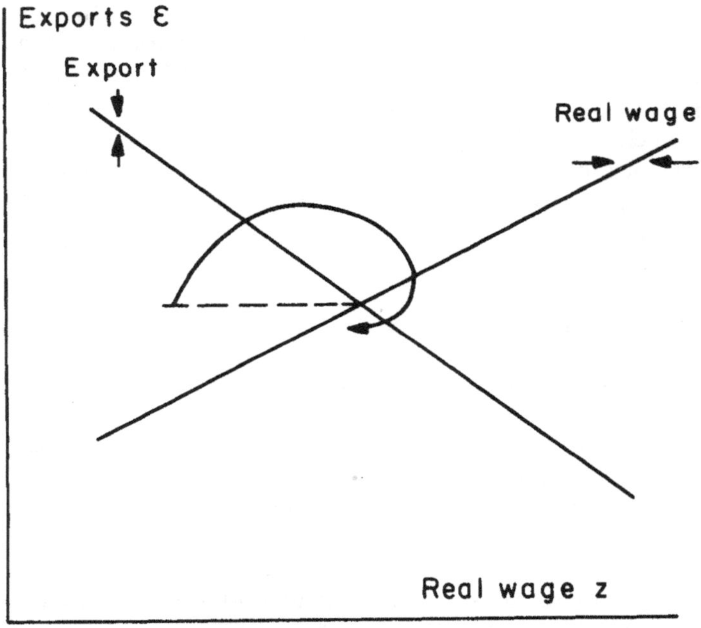

FIGURE 3 Dynamic response to a maxidevaluation. The real wage jumps down, leading to growth in exports and inflationary wage increases. The economy returns to the initial equilibrium, with overshooting and inflationary stop-go output response.

such as

$$\hat{\varepsilon} = A[\varepsilon^*(z) - \varepsilon], \tag{25}$$

where A is a parameter describing speed of adjustment. From this equation, actual exports gradually approach the level $\varepsilon^*(z)$ consistent with real wage. Together, (7) with α set to zero and (25) form a dynamic system in the real wage and exports. Taking into account the positive response of capacity utilization to ε and z (really, the negative effect apart from exports of q on u in (A.1)), loci along which $\hat{\varepsilon} = 0$ and $\hat{z} = 0$ appear in Figure 3.

From an initial equilibrium a maxi-devaluation followed by an exchange rate freeze cuts the real wage, displacing z to the left at the initial ε. Both variables begin to rise, and ultimately spiral back to equilibrium, perhaps with overshooting (as shown). The activity level first drops, and then also will follow a spiral path. Inflation jumps up, and then declines in fits and starts as workers regain their target real wage. Stop-and-go inflationary output fluctuations follow in the wake of the maxi—small wonder that policy-makers treat such policies with distaste. A smoother move might be to step up the rate of a crawling peg, which shifts the real wage locus to the left. A long-term export gain is the result, stimulating demand but cutting the real wage.

3. ALTERNATIVE MACROECONOMIC CLOSURES

Output or capacity utilization is the key macroeconomic adjustment variable in the model discussed so far, along the lines urged by Kalecki and the Keynes of the *General Theory*. Output adjustment is plausible in many instances, especially during the contractionary stabilization programs which developing countries often undergo. Nonetheless, alternative adjustment modes and other sectors and financial instruments should be considered, since they apply in a wide range of circumstances. We pursue both tracks in this chapter. The aim of the exercises is to show how the basic model framework can be extended to deal with institutional structures and policy issues that arise frequency in the Third World.

Regarding adjustment modes, we first work through a model presupposing full capacity utilization, which gives monetarist results. We then go on to consider problems posed by strict limits on foreign borrowing, as in the well-known two-gap specification. Policy difficulties of a different kind can arise from a foreign exchange bonanza, when a country has not too little to spend abroad, but too much. One arrives at models of the "Dutch disease" in which the relative price of traded and non-traded goods gets out of line. Such an adjustment story is taken up here in a "fix/flex price" model in which an industrial sector with mark-up pricing relies for intermediate inputs upon a sector with an inelastic supply of products (energy, transport, etc.) which are not internationally traded. The intermediate price can vary in inflationary fashion to clear the market. The chapter closes with an analysis of why interest rate reform is unlikely to generate true credit expansion, even in a financial system in which non-productive assets (call them "gold") make up a substantial proportion of private portfolios.

3.1. Monetarism

Making sense of monetarism is tricky in a full macro model like that set out in chapter 2. On the whole, monetarists ascribe inflationary phenomena to excess demands for output and/or certain assets, ignoring cost-based explanations of price change while holding capacity utilization constant. In effect, inflation adjusts to make excess demand disappear. This view has a long history, pre-dating the controversy between the English Currency and Banking Schools 150 years ago. Present-day applied monetarism follows what Amadeo [1] calls the "Post-Wicksellian synthesis" associated with Dennis Robertson, the Keynes of the *Treatise on Money* and the 1930's Stockholm School of Swedes. The key assumptions are that u is fixed, and that banks create credit to make loans for investment demand, while the public has to absorb the corresponding liability.

Let loans be the only bank asset, while liabilities are desired deposits plus undesired ones—call the latter "money" and assume that it alone generates inflation. Monetary policy enters this model in exogenous fashion, affecting the interest rate. However, the supply of bank liabilities (desired plus undesired holdings of "money") is endogenous, determined by the level of outstanding bank assets or credit.

To see how a cumulative inflation process works, we can assume with Wicksell that desired saving (= new bank deposits) and investment (= new bank loans) depend on the interest rate. If the rate is pegged too low, the demand for new loans exceeds the desired increase in saving supply. Investment plans are realized, so the public is forced off its desired saving schedule, accumulating money balances in addition to deposits. In algebra,

$$\text{Desired saving} = s(i)\tau BX,$$

$$\text{Desired investment} = g(i)\tau BX,$$

and

$$\text{Increase in money} = \dot{M} = [g(i) - s(i)]\tau BX. \qquad (26)$$

Where does the increase in money stock go? It must be taken up by the public, willingly or not. If the latter, realized consumption becomes $PC = wbX + (1-s)\tau BX - \dot{M}$, less than planned by $\dot{M}$ when i is held low enough to make g exceed s.

Maintaining the hypothesis that people are forced off their desired consumption schedules, let us also assume that the equation of exchange applies for undesired deposits, $MV = PK$, where V is treated not as a state variable but as an increasing function of inflation $\hat{P}$. Differentiating with respect to time gives $\hat{P} = \dot{M}V/PK$, and substitution into (26) gives the growth rate formula

$$g = s + \frac{1+\tau}{\tau u}\frac{\hat{P}}{V(\hat{P})}, \tag{27}$$

so that investment (or net government spending or exports) can exceed desired saving insofar as it is financed by the "inflation tax" appearing in the last term. If V rises with $\hat{P}$, the "base" of the tax is oviously eroded by faster inflation. Monetarists make a great deal of this point. Structuralists make another about distribution, as we will see immediately below and in section 5.1.

The notion that the public may be forced off its desired consumption schedule is not congenial to neoclassicals, who like rational foundations for people's acts. They are easy to provide in this case. The instantaneous loss of the value of one's real balances M/P from inflation is measured by $\dot{P}(M/P)$ where $\dot{P}$ is the absolute change in prices. If real wealth is reduced by this quantity, why not make it good by increased saving? *Desired* consumption becomes $PC = wbX + (1-s)\tau bX - \hat{P}M$, if the inflation rate is rationally expected or perfectly foreseen. Using this expression for consumption together with the equation of exchange gives rise to (27)—the inflation tax is rationally paid.

To translate this Wicksell process into the accounting of Chapter 2, we simply assume that consumer demand in (10) or (18) responds negatively to inflation rates, from the inflation tax for example. The hypothesis may not be empirically plausible (especially if money is largely indexed), but it generates a stable adjustment in commodity markets. Let the level of activity be fixed at "full capacity." Then, if an incipient excess of investment over saving occurs, inflation will speed up, aggregate demand will fall and equilibrium will be re-established.

Since interest rate increases also reduce demand, this story underlies a negatively sloped relationship between i and $\hat{P}$ in

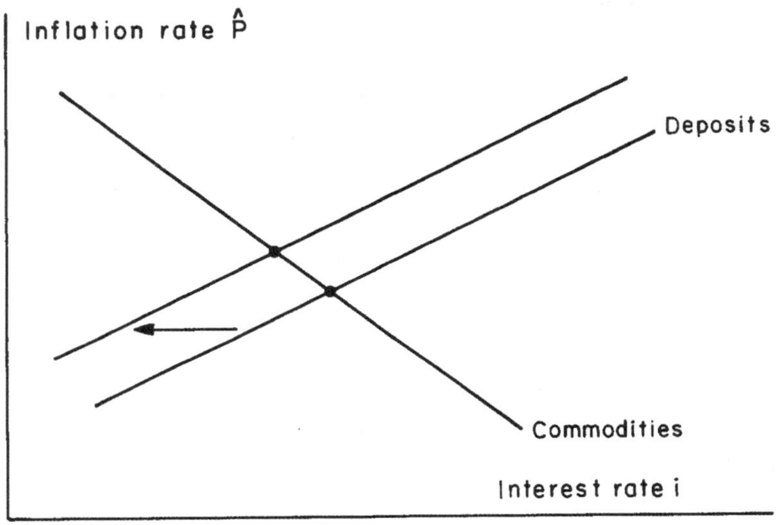

FIGURE 4 Monetarist interpretation of expansionary monetary policy. The interest rate falls, stimulating aggregate demand. To maintain macro equilibrium, the inflation rate has to rise to choke the incipient expansion off.

commodity markets, as shown in Figure 4. With indexed deposits, an increase in $\hat{P}$ causes i to rise in the deposit equation, as also shown. A higher credit multiplier μ or lower velocity V makes the interest rate fall, shifting the Deposit schedule leftward. Inflation goes up, choking off any increase in aggregate demand, and the attempted monetary expansion is purely inflationary. In contrast, a monetary crunch is a good way to get inflation down. A good way to push it up is through fiscal expansion (with an increased PSBR) whch shifts the commodity locus upward.

Hidden hypotheses lurk in the background. Since we know they work the wrong way for monetarism, Cavallo/Patman interest rate cost-push effects are left out. Capacity utilization u is fixed, or at least does not affect saving and investment. The inflation rate can jump in the short run, which means from (3) that τ, w, or e must also jump. We have to give up a behavioral explanation of cost as a counterpart to setting the variable u exogenously. Finally, since $V = P_K K/F$ is a state variable, we cannot assume that it is a function of the inflation rate but have to worry about its dynamics over time.

Interesting results about the distributional implications of monetary policy follow, as we will see.

Suppose that $\hat{\tau}$ jumps to meet changes in $\hat{P}$ as determined in Figure 4, i.e., we abandon Eq. (4). The authorities also adroitly adjust the exchange rate to meet domestic inflation—$\hat{e}$ equals $\hat{P}$ and the real rate q stays constant. For present purposes it is interesting to carry along the inflation pass-through coefficient κ discussed in connection with Eq. (7) explicitly. The real wage growth rate equation becomes

$$\hat{z} = -\lambda(z - \bar{z}) - (1 - \kappa)\hat{P}. \tag{28}$$

When $\hat{e} = \hat{P}$, the growth rate of velocity becomes $\hat{V} = \hat{P} + g - \hat{F}$. The inflation rate $\hat{P}$ and the capital stock growth rate g are determined by the short run model—for present purposes they depend on μ and V. If we ignore international reserves, taxes, and export subsidies in (23), we have $\hat{F} = (\gamma + qt)V + i$, so that fiscal debt rises with government spending, the trade surplus, and the interest rate. The growth rate of velocity is therefore

$$\hat{V} = \hat{P}(\mu, V) + g(\mu, V) - [\gamma + qt(\mu, V)]V - i. \tag{29}$$

Here, an increase in V reduces $\hat{V}$, by cutting $\hat{P}$ and increasing the real interest rate (reducing g), as well as directly through the bracketed term multiplying V. The system (28) and (29) is a stable pair of differential equations for $\hat{z}$ and $\hat{V}$. Since the monetarist model makes inflation independent of cost pressures through the wage, $\hat{V}$ is independent of z.

Figure 5 illustrates adjustment between steady states at which $\hat{V} = \hat{z} = 0$. A permanently higher credit multiplier μ raises the inflation rate from Figure 4. Hence to hold $\hat{V} = 0$ in (29), V must rise. In (28), holding $\hat{z} = 0$ requires z to fall. One outcome in a new steady state is a higher value of V. Since fiscal debt creation $\hat{F}$ is proportional to V, we also have faster growth of base money. These predictions are in line with monetarist orthodoxy but here they arise from evolutionary change in a state variable, not simple portfolio shifts.

As far as real wages are concerned, z will be lower in the new steady state unless κ or λ has a "high" value. For z to rise, either wage increases must be tightly linked to price changes or workers must be able to force wage inflation when their real wage declines in

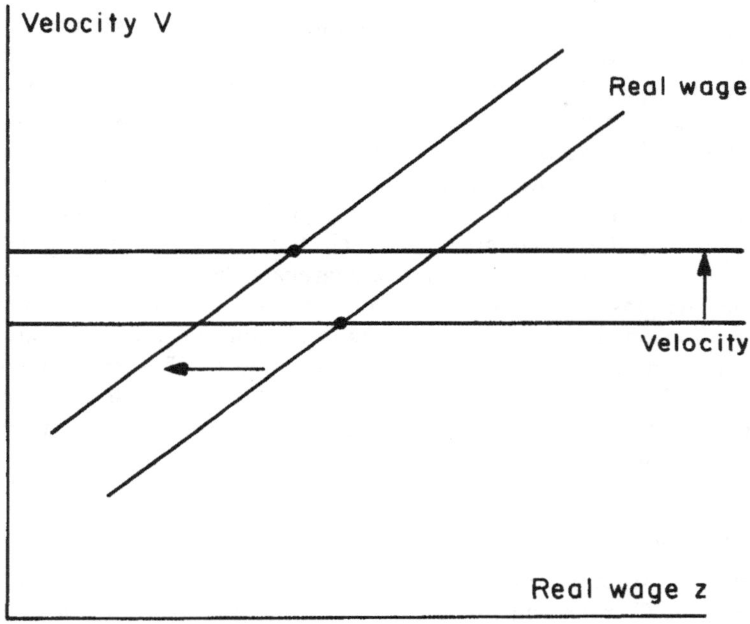

FIGURE 5 Long-term effects of monetary expansion. Across compared steady states, velocity shifts upward and the real wage down. In the final outcome, the real wage can either rise or fall, depending on how well workers can defend themselves against erosion of their real purchasing power.

the short run. Lacking such powers, labor will be hurt in the long run by money-induced price inflations. This is the forced saving mechanism stressed by the post-Wicksellians.

Inflation reduction is often pursued by reducing the credit multiplier μ. Even in a monetarist world, the effectiveness of such programs is enhanced if workers' power to resist real wage cuts is curtailed. In Figure 5, a lower μ will shift the curves opposite to the arrows. The real wage might tend to rise, *except* that reductions in κ and λ may be imposed by statutory or institutional change. The effect from (28) is to reduce the slope of the real wage locus, offsetting its rightward shift. Lower inflation as signalled by reduced velocity is achieved at the cost of lower real wages—convergence to a new steady state is faster because forced saving (slower wage than price inflation) makes aggregate demand decline by shifting the income distribution in favor of profits. This is the structuralist interpretation of monetarist stabilization.

Do these results carry over to less restricted models? In Section 5.4 we take up the question of regime shifts, after showing for our basic model in Sections 5.1–5.3 that results of a monetarist flavor persist if we reinstate capacity utilization as the macro adjusting variable and assume that α is strongly positive in (4). From either perspective, the monetarist approach boils down to saying that inflation responds sharply to more aggregate demand via increased profit margins, and also rapidly chokes any increase in capacity utilization off. Moreover, as we saw in Section 2.6 a large positive value of α offsets the Cavallo/Patman effect. This story hangs together logically, although it is questionable how well it fits the data. Other views are certainly possible, as we will see in the following chapters.

3.2. External strangulation

'External strangulation' was a phrase used around the UN Economic Commission for Latin America in the 1960's to describe the state of economies subject to extreme shortages of foreign exchange. The malady is widespread in the 1980's after the debt crisis and stagnation of foreign aid—Finance Ministers and Central Bankers scramble for every penny. In this section, we describe some of the symptoms of strangulation, on both the real and financial sides of the economy.

Suppose that the trade surplus t is specified exogenously, say from a strict limit by bankers on the amount that can be borrowed externally. Fixing t amounts to adding a restriction to the model of Chapter 2; as with the imposition of unchanging capacity utilization in the monetarist model, we have to find another degree of freedom. Several possibilites arise.

One is simply to solve (16) and (17) for u and $\hat{P}$ as functions of t. The rationale is that scarce foreign resources cause bottlenecks and inflationary pressure in the domestic economy, a point developed further in a two-sector model in Section 3.3. A dollar inflow would let t decline and u rise. The Commodity locus in Figure 4 would shift downward, with less inflation as an outcome. Attempts to stabilize inflation may depend critically on access to foreign exchange because of this linkage, as we will see in Section 4.5.

A second adjustment scenario can be based on reduced public spending. Policy practice suggests that when a resource crunch arrives, public investment suffers—projects are easier to cut back than the salary of a teacher or bureaucrat. State investment (per unit of capital) becomes a new endogenous variable, say j. Overall capital growth becomes

$$g = j + g_0(\tau) + h\beta u - h(i - \hat{P}),$$

where the latter terms follow from private investment as in (12).

With this extension, the aggregate balance Eq. (18) is

$$\{c_0 + \gamma + \theta[j + g_0 + h\beta u - h(i - \hat{P})]\}$$
$$- \left\{\left[\frac{s\tau}{(1+\tau)(1+v)} + \frac{si\omega + \phi}{(1+\tau)(1+v)(1+i\omega)} + \frac{v}{1+v}\right]u - \varepsilon\right\} = 0. \tag{30}$$

The first term in curly brackets in (30) is the demand injection from within the economy—the constant term in the consumption function plus current and capital spending by the state plus private investment. The other term in curly brackets shows saving. Sources are mark-up and interest income, intermediate imports, indirect taxes, and exports as a negative (dis-saving) item. After feedbacks through i and $\hat{P}$ are taken into account, the overall stability condition is that the total derivative of the first bracketed term with respect to u should be smaller than the derivative of the second one—the demand injection should respond less strongly to activity than saving supply.

The stability requirement is respected by the slopes of the Demand injection and Saving supply schedules in Figure 6. The loci for Total imports in the diagram show that a given import bill is made up of capital goods and intermediates to support production—if one component rises, the other must fall.

If there is no foreign trade constraint, the model is driven in the direction of the arrows by increased demand from government current spending γ or capital formation j. Capacity utilization increases along the saving schedule, and total imports rise. If imports must be curtailed due to a foreign exchange bottleneck the

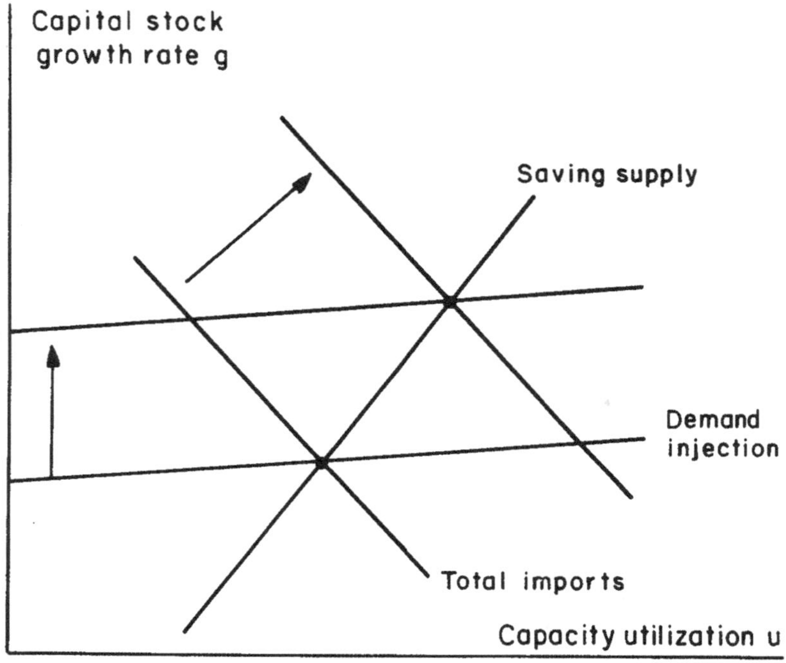

FIGURE 6 Macro adjustment involving trade. A demand injection increases capacity utilization and the growth rate if total imports can increase. In another causal pattern, a cut in imports can force less demand by curtailing government capital formation (the schedules move opposite to the arrows).

schedules shift the other way. Government investment turns into an endogenous variable, and its reduction permits the demand injection locus to shift downward. Along the lines of the classic two-gap paper by Chenery and Bruno [9], one can show that $dj/dt < -1$, or an increase in the trade surplus forces a greater than one-for-one reduction in government investment. The reason is that the import content of capital formation is the fraction $1 - \theta$. Cutting foreign resources forces investment to be cut by even more—for the algebra see Taylor [40] or Bacha [3].

Diagrams like Figure 6 can also be used to illustrate "export-led growth." (The label should be attached in practice to any activity—say import substitution—that saves or generates foreign resources.)

The case in which there is no binding import constraint appears in the upper part of Figure 7. By reducing foreign saving *ex ante* a higher export proportion ε shifts the Saving supply schedule downward. Private investment responds to capacity utilization and goes up.

In the lower diagram, there is a binding import constraint and state capital formation becomes endogenous. Higher exports shift the Saving function downward, as before. But they also permit a higher import level, shifting that schedule outward. Public investment rises to equilibrate the trade and saving gaps.

Sources of growth besides export expansion can also be illustrated with these diagrams. Greater current state spending would shift the Demand injection locus upward in the upper diagram, stimulating growth. But the strategy would not work if there were a binding import restriction (the import schedule could not shift out). As Dutt [12] points out, income redistribution from high-saving profit recipients to low-saving workers looks like an export expansion in the upper diagram by shifting the saving schedule down. However, unless the direct-and-indirect import basket of workers were much smaller than that of capitalists, the outward shift of the import locus in the trade-constrained lower diagram would not be sufficient to let growth speed up.

On the financial side of the model, the easiest way to deal with external strangulation is to assume that F^*, the growth rate of the state's foreign obligations, is predetermined. Ignoring reserve changes, (22) then shows that

$$t = (F^*/K)(i^* - \hat{F}^*), \tag{31}$$

so that a reduction in $\hat{F}^*$ forces the trade surplus to rise. Indeed, for many developing countries in the mid-1980's, $i^* > \hat{F}^*$, so that they have to run positive trade balances.

Again omitting reserves, the growth rate $\hat{F}$ of domestic debt from (23) becomes

$$\hat{F} = V\left(\frac{P}{P_k}\right)\left(\gamma + j - \frac{v}{1-v}u\right) + f(i^* - \hat{F}^*) + i \tag{32}$$

Here, slower growth in foreign debt (or a greater trade surplus from (31)) apparently forces domestic borrowing to speed up. However, the argument in connection with Figure 6 suggests that a higher t

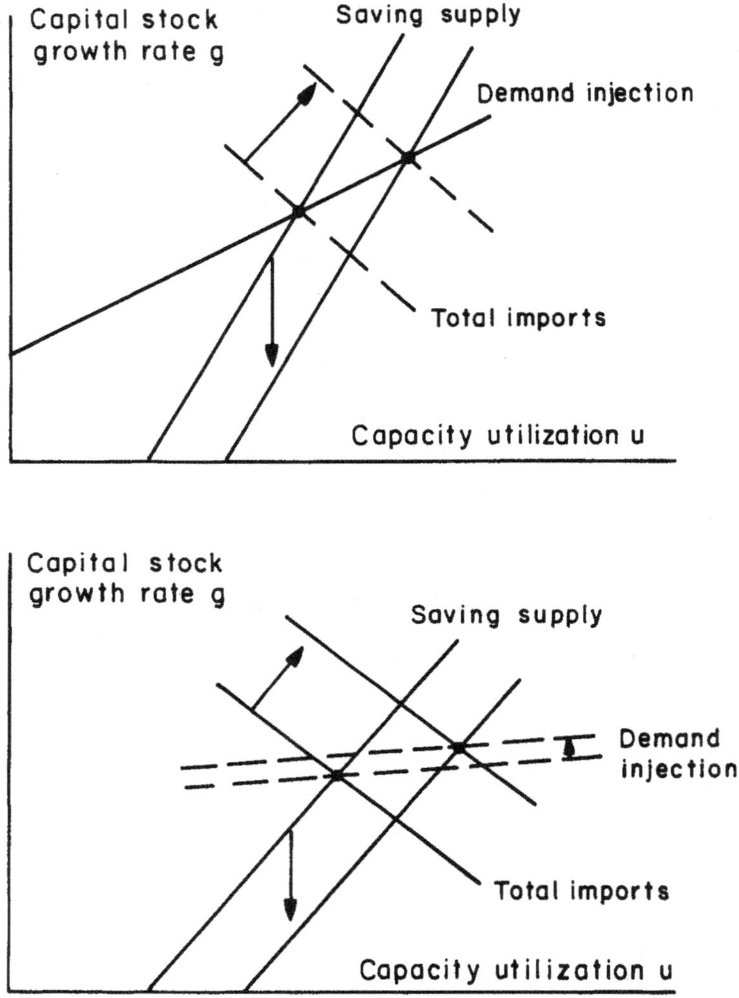

FIGURE 7 Export-led growth under two circumstances. In the upper diagram, without an import constraint, reduced *ex ante* saving increases growth in Keynesian fashion. In the lower diagram, faster growth depends upon the fact that greater exports permit total imports to rise.

makes government investment j decline more than one-for-one. Hence, a reduction in F^* would make growth slow down enough to permit the internal public sector borrowing requirement to fall!

This conclusion perhaps shows that results from models should not be taken too literally. What occurs in the real world is that a binding trade constraint can be met by many devices—forced import substitution (reducing the import coefficient a in (1)), reduction of inventories, policy changes such as imposition of quotas, even finding oil. All these moves plus reduced public capital formation help the economy reach a higher level of t, and all will have different implications for fiscal spending. The cut in investment is the one that will affect the borrowing requirement most. In the mid-1980s, some countries like Brazil have pursued export promotion and import substitution so aggressively in wake of the debt crisis that they seem to have a structural trade surplus. From (32), finding sources of domestic borrowing to meet the excess of i^* over $\hat{F}^*$ becomes a major issue. Elsewhere, less fortunate countries may have cut government spending j so drastically that (32) is easily satisfied. The real blessing for them would be faster growth of external debt (or lower interest rates), a reduction in their required trade surpluses, and the possibility to grow again.

3.3. Flexible prices and access to foreign exchange

External strangulation of the price system deserves to be examined more fully. In a model for Nicaragua, Gibson [17] argues that industrial prices are more flexible, the tighter the external constraint binds. Suppose there is a positive demand shock, so that industrial prices rise. Since industry provides inputs to the agro-export sector, export prices go up from the side of costs, reducing external demand. Foreign exchange supply falls, limiting intermediate imports, reducing industrial output and driving up its price still more. Income effects rule out macro instability in the model, but price increases still cause policy pain.

Paradoxically, ample foreign exchange creates similar problems. Readily available dollars can lead to exchange appreciation—higher relative prices of non-traded goods. Inflation and reduced export diversity and economic activity as imports flood in are the common results. Academics rediscovered such phenomena in recent years—the result is a large literature on the "Dutch disease." Foreign aid recipients, oil exporters, and beneficiaries of unexpected upswings in their external terms of trade are the common sufferers in the Third World.

Price responses to both external strangulation and bonanzas fit into a two-sector model that development economists often use. In one sector, the price follows mark-up rules and output meets demand. The other 'flex-price' sector has inelastic output. Its price varies to equate demand and supply. Many non-traded goods are intermediates (energy, transport, etc.). They group naturally into a flex-price aggregate. Barbone's [4] compact model deals with price effects of bonanzas and strangulation. It serves double duty in illustrating the effects of import quotas in Section 4.1 below.

Supplies of intermediate inputs can come from domestic sources or imports. We carry the latter in the accounting of this section but effectively treat intermediates as non-tradable and assume that their import level $\bar{m}$ (total imports divided by the capital stock) is set exogeneously or by quota and cannot change in the short run. We do, however, permit the fixed imports to generate "rents" along the lines argued by Krueger [24] and successors.

There is a rising supply curve for domestically-produced intermediate goods of the form $m = m(P_m/w)$, where P_m is the flexible price. People who can get access to the fixed imports gain a rental income $(P_m - eP_0^*)\bar{m}$ from buying in the world market at price eP_0^* and reselling internally at P_m. Domestic producers of import substitutes get profits $(P_m - w)m$ and wage income wm is also generated in the industry.

Assume that the saving rate from rents and import substitution profits is s (the same rate as from mark-up income). Then excess demand for the home-produced good can be written as

$$c_0(\hat{P}) + (\theta + q(1-\theta)P_i^*)[g_0(\tau) - h(i - \hat{P})] + \left[\frac{(h-s)\tau}{(1+v)(1+\tau)} - \frac{v}{1+v} - \frac{si\omega}{(1+v)(1+\tau)(1+i\omega)} - s\frac{P_m}{P}a\right]u + s(zm + qP_0^*\bar{m}) + \gamma + [\varepsilon - qP_0^*\bar{m} - q(1-\theta)P_1^*g]. \quad (33)$$

This equation should be compared to (18). It contains a few more terms corresponding to saving from rents and import substitution profits, but is largely the same *except* for the inclusion of the intermediate price P_m. This input cost shows up in output price determination, since (3) should be rewritten as

$$B = wb + P_m a.$$

The model has a new variable P_m, which needs a corresponding equation. Excess demand for intermediates should vanish, or

$$au - \bar{m} - m(P_m/w) = 0. \tag{34}$$

Comparative statics of this fix/flex model are shown in Figure 8. More capacity use increases demand for the intermediate, making

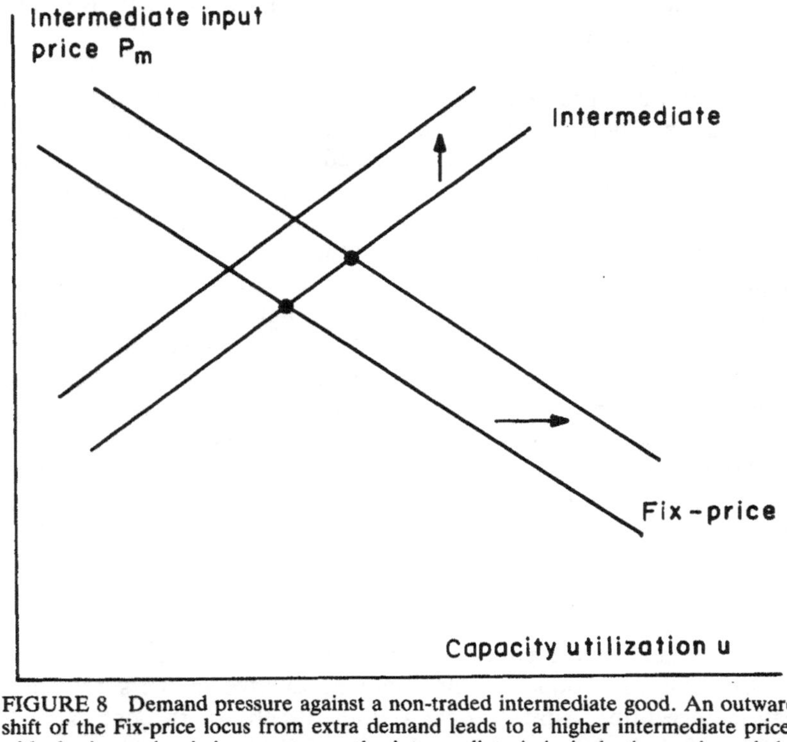

FIGURE 8 Demand pressure against a non-traded intermediate good. An outward shift of the Fix-price locus from extra demand leads to a higher intermediate price, with the increasing being greater as the intermediate is in inelastic supply and the corresponding schedule is steep. The upward shift of the Intermediate locus could result from difficulty in obtaining required imported intermediates when there is external strangulation. A higher intermediate price and potential inflation are the outcomes.

its price rise on the corresponding schedule. Its slope is steeper, the less elastic is supply. A higher P_m generates incomes for people reselling intermediate imports and for domestic producers, raising available saving. Since greater activity in the mark-up sector also creates potential saving, P_m and u trade off inversely along the Fix-price line, for given effective demand.

Scarce dollars can lead to a lower quota $\bar{m}$ and squeeze intermediate supply if producing m requires imports. Outcomes resemble those of Gibson's [17] model discussed above. The Intermediate locus shifts upward, so that P_m rises and u drops off. A foreign bonanza has different effects. Not all the extra dollars can be spent abroad, so demand for national products will rise. The Fix-price locus shifts right, and P_m goes up.

Both the upward shift of the Intermediate locus (from strangulation) and the rightward shift of the Fix-price schedule (from a bonanza) are inflationary—strangulation also makes activity drop. Were inflation the only problem caused by the bonanza, its effects might be tolerable. However, policy-makers often fell little incentive to devalue or even adopt a crawling peg; after all, foreign exchange appears not to be a problem. The outcome is real appreciation. At best, lagging exports and reverse import substitution may result; at worst, unstable dynamic process like those discussed in Sections 2.6 and 4.4 can be set off; imperiling prospects for growth in the medium run. Unless sensible policy measures like promotion of non-traditional exports, import controls, and sterilization of some part of the "free" foreign inflows are pursued, medium-term outcomes can be painful—especially after the bonanza ebbs. Wealth is a blessing, but one has to ponder how to use it well.

3.4. Financial liberalization

The assets held by the public that we have considered so far—loans to firms and bank deposits—are both productive in the sense that they finance firms' capital stocks (either directly or through banks' lending of their deposit base). However, unproductive assets such as precious objects, speculative land-holdings, etc. are visible throughout the Third World. Does their presence significantly affect how asset markets function?

The question is relevant to policy because a standard piece of orthodox advice to Third World countries is to proceed apace with financial liberalization, e.g., McKinnon [30] and Shaw [36]. The centerpiece of a program usually is a boost in interest rates, which is supposed to increase saving as well as draw resources into the banking system for productive lending. In a demand-driven system like the one we are analyzing here, higher saving would be counter-productive by reducing aggregate demand. However, this possibility is not important since econometrics by Giovannini [18] and others shows that saving is not interest-responsive in samples of developing countries in any case. The more interesting idea is that overall financial efficiency will be enhanced by higher rates. We can explore this possibility by extending the portfolio menu of Table 1 to include another asset—unproductive in the present case. The exercise leads to the interesting conclusion that financial reform emphasizing interest rate increases is likely to fail. It also illustrates another generic class of models that like the fix/flex price system discussed last section is widely applicable in developing country macro.

To set the stage, consider financial reform in the simple model underlying Eq. (20). Assume that the return to holding bank deposits is $i_d + \hat{P}$ (instead of just $\hat{P}$ as in the equations), where i_d is a controlled deposit rate. What happens when i_d is increased, as McKinnon recommends? If loans to firms and deposits are the public's only assets, the outcome is not promising. A higher i_d raises δ *ex ante,* but it can't go up *ex post* since overall deposits are limited by the supply of money in the last term of the equation. Hence, the loan rate i must rise to restore equilibrium, and firms find it more costly to get credit. Stagflation along the lines sketched in Section 1.6 would ensue. Not a promising beginning for a liberalization attempt.

Now bring in the unproductive asset y. Following Taylor [40] it can be called "gold." It has an associated, perhaps largely psychic, income stream R (how much has to be hoarded for dowries?) and a market price P_y. The rate of return to holding gold is R/P_y. If we normalize its stock by fiscal assets F, the public's total wealth is

$$W = F + eR^* + P_k K + P_y yF, \qquad (35)$$

replacing (19). Since it depends on P_y which varies to clear the gold market, W now is an endogenous variable in the short run. If χ is the share of total wealth devoted to gold holdings, that asset's demand-supply equilibrium can be written as

$$\frac{1}{P_y}\chi\left(i, i_d+\hat{P}, \frac{R}{P_y}, u\right)(V+e\rho+1+P_y y)-y=0. \qquad (36)$$

Now we have to consider the market for loans to firms. Heretofore, we have assumed that strict reserve requirements apply to the banking system, with deposits D tied to base money H by the rule $D=\mu H$. Loan supply from banks is therefore $D-H=(\mu-1)H$. This formulation is convenient, but ignores the fact that what bankers really do is look at their deposit base, and *choose* to lend out some fraction ξ of it. It is reasonable to suppose that ξ rises with the loan rate i, but stays less than unity because of prudence, reserve requirements, etc. In the notation of Table 1, bank loan supply is

$$\frac{L_b}{F}=\xi(i)\delta\left(i, i_d+\hat{P}, \frac{R}{P_y}, u\right)(V+e\rho+1+P_y y),$$

where δ is the public's deposit function. The public's loan supply is

$$\frac{L_p}{F}=(1-\delta-\chi)(V+e\rho+1+P_y y)$$

while firms' total loan demand scaled by fiscal debt is $P_k K/F=V$. (For simplicity we do not consider equity finance or the possibility that firms may have non-zero net worth.)

The demand-supply balance for loans from these equations is

$$V-[(1-\delta-\chi)+\xi\delta](V+e\rho+1+P_y y)=0. \qquad (37)$$

From (37) it is easy to see that increases in δ and χ make the excess demand for loans to go up, leading i to rise. Higher bank reserves ($1+e\rho$ when scaled by F) and lower velocity reduce excess demand and the interest rate.

Equations (36) and (37) jointly determine the loan rate i and the gold price P_y. An increase in the deposit rate i_d or the inflation rate $\hat{P}$ will lead deposit demand δ to go up and gold demand χ to decline. At the same time, the public's loans to firms $1-\delta-\chi$ will go down as well. If the asset shift "mostly" comes from gold, will total loan supply from the public and the banks' increased deposit base go up? If so, interest rate increases for deposits will be a productive policy move.

After a bit of manipulation, the effect of $\hat{P}$ (or i_d) on i can be shown to be proportional to

$$\frac{RW}{(P_y)^2}(1-\xi)\left[\delta_R\chi_R\left(\frac{\delta_{\hat{P}}}{\delta_R}-\frac{\chi_{\hat{P}}}{\chi_R}\right)\right]+(1-\xi)y[\delta\chi_{\hat{P}}+(1-\chi)\delta_{\hat{P}}]$$

where subscripts denote partial derivatives. From this expression, one can see that i will fall if

$$-\frac{\delta_{\hat{P}}}{\chi_{\hat{P}}}<-\frac{\delta_R}{\chi_R}\text{ and/or }-\frac{\delta_{\hat{P}}}{\chi_{\hat{P}}}<\frac{\delta}{1-\chi}$$

The first inequality describes substitution effects. Normally, one would expect $-\delta_{\hat{P}}/\chi_{\hat{P}}>1>-\delta_R/\chi_R$. The term $\delta_{\hat{P}}$ is an own-derivative for deposit demand with respect to inflation and/or the deposit rate, while $\chi_{\hat{P}}$ is a cross-derivative. If own-responses are stronger than cross-responses, the ratio should exceed unity, while $-\delta_R/\chi_R$ (a ratio of cross- to own-response) should be less than one. Only if rentiers move out of gold into *loans* when the deposit rate goes up (or from deposits at least partly into loans when the gold return goes up) will the first inequality be satisfied.

The second inequality describes wealth effects. Since $\delta/(1-\chi)<1$ (part of wealth is held in loans) one also needs the odd response to changes in deposit rates for it to hold. These asset demand patterns are possible, but it would take strong empirical evidence or institutional arguments to make one deem them likely to occur. Even if the public gives no loans to firms at all, the reasoning above goes through since changes in δ and χ must be mutually offsetting when $\delta+\chi=1$. In this case, one can show that i is independent of i_d since insertion of (36) into (37) gives $V-\xi(i)(V+e\rho+1)=0$ as the loan market equilibrium condition.

Factors that may save the liberalization argument are market segmentation so that loans from the public carry a higher interest rate than loans from banks, or a possible *positive* dependence of ξ on i_d (so that if deposits are made more expensive to banks, they loosen up their lending operation). A quantitative assessment of these possibilities would have to be made on institutional grounds—superficially, they do not appear promising.

Considerations like the ones just presented suggest that the argument for raising interest rates to energize a repressed financial system is not well-founded. In any case, interest rate reform has been taken over by events. Especially in developing countries open to the international financial system, the problem today is not excessively low real rates but excessively high ones. How they might be brought down is the topic of Sections 4.4 and 4.5 below.

3.5. Summary on alternative closures and extensions to the basic model

The morals that can be drawn from this chapter are as follows:

1) 'Closure' of the basic model, or the specification of binding macro constraints and directions of causality, affects the *directions* of results that it produces. If the economy is foreign exchange-constrained, for example, it performs in a qualitatively different fashion than when it is not. In practice, this finding means that one should be clear about the closure assumptions one builds into models, to avoid slipping in predictions about outcomes by fiat. The decision about closure rules almost has to be made on institutional and conjunctural grounds—directions of causality in the past are not easily discerned by econometrics and in any case may change tomorrow. Monetarism is a good example of how model outcomes can be predetermined by closure assumptions. This point is further developed in Chapter 5.

2) A developing economy often has micro structure in the sense that key macroeconomic phenomena may be obscured if the system is treated as a one commodity/one financial market aggregate. Price-quantity interactions between fix-price and flex-price sectors are often crucial, as are financial assets besides money and loans to firms or 'bonds.' Applications have been developed here involving non-traded goods and "gold", and further examples are presented in the following chapter. Again, the choice of appropriate disaggregations requires common sense and institutional awareness. Mere facility with algebra or econometrics does not get one very far in trying to apply models to the real world.

4. MACRO ADJUSTMENT IN THE SHORT RUN

In this chapter, we take up tools that may be useful in short run policy formulation, especially external or inflation stabilization attempts. The topics covered are export subsidies and import quotas, food subsidies and food price inflation, public sector pricing, and orthodox and heterodox anti-inflationary shocks.

4.1. Export subsidies and import quotas

The discussion in Section 2.6 makes clear that devaluation has repercussions throughout the economy—in commodity and financial markets and on the inflationary process. Are there ways in which its beneficial influences can be captured, without the problems?

'Partial' devaluations in the form of commercial policy interventions are means to this end. They require greater administrative effort than simple revision of the exchange rate, and must be designed to be institutionally feasible in a world of conflicting interest groups and seekers for rents. Nonetheless, subsidies and quotas in principle avoid some of devaluation's unfavorable effects, and their macroeconomic implications deserve to be explored. We take up two examples here—subsidies to exports and (in an extension of the basic model) import quotas.

An export subsidy is easy to deal with, since it already appears in the accounting of Chapter 2. First note that subsidizing exports does not directly affect the general price level or its inflation rate in (2) and (6), nor does it influence asset markets. Hence, one can just consider what happens when the subsidy rate ζ increases in (16) and (17). In a diagram like the top one in Figure 1, the internal balance locus shifts to the right (aggregate demand rises) and the external balance shifts upward. Since there is no real income drag from the effects of devaluation on real wages or intermediate import costs, capacity utilization unambiguously rises. With plausible values for the multiplier and intermediate import content of output, the trade balance will improve as well. The inflation and interest rates increase along the slopes of their respective schedules in Figure 1, but the schedules themselves do not shift outward. Export subsidies improve the current account and are expansionary, without bad side-effects on the interest rate and inflation. Their problem is that in a global game under unlucky conditions they can lead to trade warfare. The episode that broke out around the North Atlantic in the 1930's led directly to contemporary condemnation of export subsidies by the GATT. But, within limits, potential international economic conflict does not make such policies foolish for individual developing economies.

Import quotas are more complicated analytically. Their macroeconomic ramifications have not been widely discussed, although there is an enormous literature in trade theory damning them on rent-seeking and efficiency-loss grounds. In development economics, trade theorists shifting to policy advice in the 1970's stressed the allegedly beneficial effects of lifting quotas. Nonetheless, in Krueger's [25] well-known survey of country experiences, only four of 22 episodes of devaluation-*cum*-liberalization ("phase III liberalization" in her terminology) did not result in a fall in output, faster inflation, or renewed balance of payments problems. We already know why devaluation can have such consequences. It makes sense to look into the macroeconomics of quota liberalization.

Recent papers on the topic include Ocampo [34] and Barbone [4], with the former concentrating on direct quantity effects of import quotas on production and demand, and the latter emphasizing price linkages. Their results are complementary but we follow Barbone here for compactness of exposition. Indeed, his real-side model has already been presented as (33) and (34) in the Section 3.3 discussion of foreign strangulation and bonanzas. Comparative statics of quota liberalization (or an increase in the import quota $\bar{m}$) appear in Figure 9. The slopes of the curves can be explained as follows: Higher capacity utilization increases demand for the import substitute and causes its price to rise along the Quota schedule. At the same time, a higher price P_m generates incomes for quota-holders and import substituting entrepreneurs, raising available saving. To maintain macro equilibrium, less saving from mark-ups on commodity production is required. Hence, P_m and capacity utilization u trade off inversely along the Internal balance line.

The effects of raising the import quota $\bar{m}$ are shown by the shifts in the curves. In the internal market at the initial price P_m, aggregate demand falls since higher *ex ante* saving comes from a greater volume of quota rents. At the same time, the intermediate

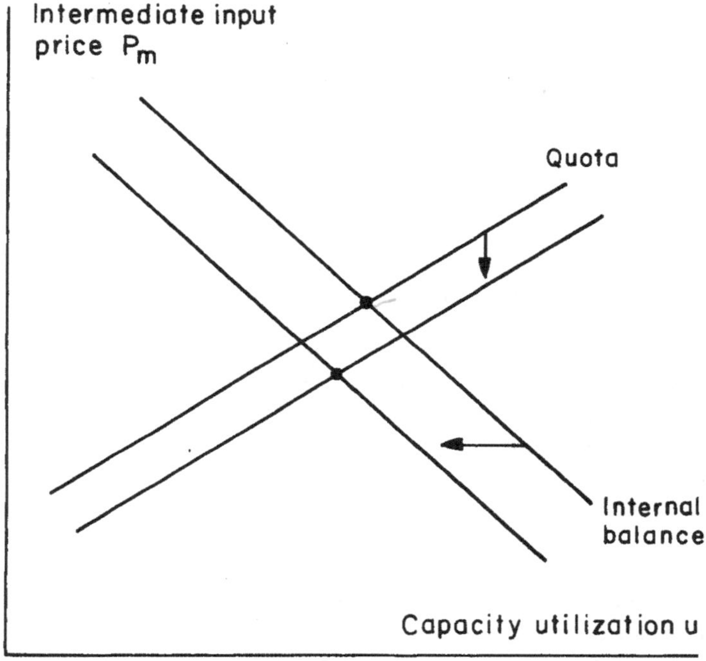

FIGURE 9 Effects of quota liberalization for intermediate imports. Initially, a greater quota generates increased rental income for import license-holders, leading potential saving to rise and the output level consistent with internal balance to decline. Simultaneously, excess supply in the intermediate goods market makes the price P_m fall. The outcome involves a lower P_m and a reduced level of activity unless P_m goes down sharply due to a low elasticity of domestic supply. Contraction could also be offset by a high elasticity of exports to a lower domestic price level resulting from cheaper intermediate input costs.

price P_m falls due to excess supply. Both changes lead to a lower P_m, but the net effect on aggregate demand is unclear. Capacity utilization u will decline unless P_m falls sharply, leading to lower final prices, an increased real wage and a strong export response. Expansion requires a *low* supply elasticity in import substitution (so that a slight decline in sales volume leads to a big price drop) or a high elasticity of export demand. There is no particular reason to expect these conditions to apply.

Devaluation also has interesting effects in this model. Since intermediate imports are limited by quota and price-responsiveness of capital goods imports is likely to be weak, exchange depreciation can only improve the current account on the side of exports. The condition is that the export demand elasticity should exceed unity. For higher output, the export elasticity must exceed the intermediate import/export ratio, as in Section 2.3. In practice, either lower bound on the elasticity may or may not be satisfied. Finally, P_m and therefore the final output price P will fall if devaluation is contractionary (the internal balance schedule shifts leftward in Figure 9) and will rise otherwise. Following Krueger [24], orthodox economists (especially IMF mission heads in Africa) often assert that when quotas are rampant, devaluation will not be inflationary since it wipes out rents. In the present model, this pleasant circumstance occurs only when domestic activity is also wiped out. It is not clear that the inflation benefit exceeds the capacity utilization cost.

A final set of effects of quota liberalization takes place in financial markets. Barbone [4] points out that since rights to an import quota generate an income flow, control over the quota amounts to an asset. In practice, there may be markets in quotas, and they can be used as loan collaterals, etc. For simplicity, we will assume an explicit market here, in which quota rights (per unit of fiscal debt) y sell for a price P_y. The return R to holding a quota is given by

$$\frac{P_m - eP_0^*}{P_y} = \frac{R}{P_y}$$

Quota rights act as a third asset in a variant of the model incorporating "gold" in Section 3.4. If for simplicity we revert to the assumption that bank deposits are strictly tied to base money ($D = \mu H$), asset demand balances can be written for deposits

$$\delta(i, \hat{P}, R/P_y, u)(V + e\rho + 1 + P_y y) = \mu(1 + e\rho) \qquad (38)$$

and for quota rights,

$$(1/P_y)\chi(i, \hat{P}, R/P_y, u)(V + e\rho + 1 + P_y y) = y. \qquad (39)$$

The interest rate i and the asset price P_y are the adjusting variables in (38) and (39). Comparative statics in the quota rent case appear in Figure 10.

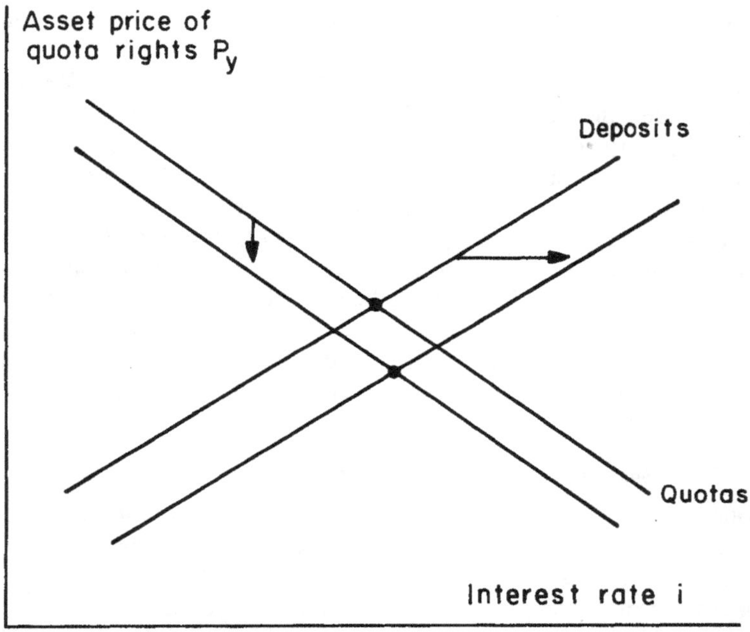

FIGURE 10 Financial market equilibrium when rights to import quotas are an asset. By increasing the availability of quotas and reducing the price of importables, liberalization leads the asset price of quota rights to fall and may cause the interest rate to rise. The latter effect can exacerbate the contractionary effect of liberalization.

The Deposit locus corresponding to (38) in the figure slopes upward, since a higher price P_y for quota rights increases wealth and reduces the return to holding quotas. Rentiers demand more deposits and drive up the rate of interest. The Quota locus slopes downward, since a higher interest rate pulls asset demand toward loans, causing the stock price for quota rights to fall.

A fall in the import price P_m or an increase in quotas $\bar{m}(=F/K)y$ (in the present set-up) from liberalization affects both schedules the same way. A lower P_m reduces the return R and shifts asset demand away from quota rights, leading the Deposit curve to move to the right as interest rates rise; the quota schedule shifts down as the price P_y declines. More quota rights initially bid up i by creating wealth and reduce P_y to clear the market. The outcomes of both shifts are lower P_y and under appropriate circumstances a higher interest rate i.

These financial adjustments have real consequences. We have already seen in connection with (33) and (34) that liberalization in the form of raising $\bar{m}$ may be associated with a lower intermediate input price P_m and reduced activity. In financial markets these changes lower the return to holding quotas and can bid up the interest rate, further cutting demand. On both the financial and real sides of the economy, lifting quotas is problematic in the short run. Regardless of its advertised efficiency benefits, an exercise in liberalization can prove self-defeating by liquidating wealth and inducing recession before favorable results appear. Long-run effects may also be counter-productive, as argued in Taylor [43].

4.2. Food subsidies and food price inflation

Consumer food subsidies are a major source of contention between developing country governments and external designers of stabilization programs. Their macroeconomic effects are undoubted, since they may comprise a "large" share of government spending (say ten or twenty percent) and affect commodities that account for up to half of domestic production and consumption. Since markets for staple commodities are usually price-clearing, it make sense to analyze subsidy macroeconomics in a fix/flex specification like the one used for intermediate inputs and import quotas. Supply of food will be limited by production plus imports in the short run and income flows will be different from those in the import substitution case, but the basic logic of the model is the same. The original formulation of food sector problems along fix/flex lines was perhaps due to Kalecki [22]. The present treatment follows Taylor [40].

In principle, we should distinguish at least three prices for the "food" commodity—the price producers receive, the subsidized price that some or all consumers pay (the producer price plus processing and distribution margins less the subsidy), and the import price. Almost all governments intervene to stabilize and separate these prices, because of their strong effects on distribution. To exemplify the main effects of subsidy programs, we deal here with a case in which the government applies a percentage subsidy to reduce the food purchase price for all consumers. That is, some official agency acquires food from domestic producers or imports, and resells it to consumers at a fixed fraction of the internal producers' price. For simplicity, we ignore distribution margins.

The non-food sector is assumed to be quantity-clearing. Its equilibrium will be described by an equation like (18). Let Ω stand for the marginal saving propensity from non-food production (a term like the one in brackets multiplying u in (18)). Call the producer price of food P_j and its domestic supply (divided by the non-food sector capital stock) j. If s_j is the saving propensity from income generated in the food sector, overall consumer spending c (ignoring the intercept c_0) is

$$c = (1 - \Omega)u + (1 - s_j)P_j j.$$

We now have to consider consumer demands c_j and c_n for products of the agricultural and non-agricultural sectors. The simplest possible functions are

$$Pc_n = vc - \pi\sigma P_j$$

for non-food, and

$$P_j c_j = (1 - v)c + \pi\sigma P_j$$

for food with σP_j as the subsidized price (that is, the consumer price is a fraction σ of the producer price P_j). The constant term π represents a "floor" level of food consumption that is insensitive to price. When $\pi > 0$, it is easy to show that the share of the budget devoted to food purchases declines as total consumption c rises, in agreement with Engel's Law.

The demand-supply balance for food is $c_j - j - m_j = 0$, where m_j stands for food imports (assumed to come in via a marketing board or under a quota). After substitution from the demand functions, this relationship becomes

$$\frac{(1 - v)(1 - \Omega)}{\sigma}u + \left[\left(-1 + \frac{(1 - v)(1 - s_j)}{\sigma}\right)j - m_j + \pi\right]P_j = 0. \quad (40)$$

The excess demand function for non-food will resemble (18), with appropriate modifications to take into account food producers' income flows and the breakdown of consumer demands by sector.

Comparative statics for this model are illustrated in Figure 11.

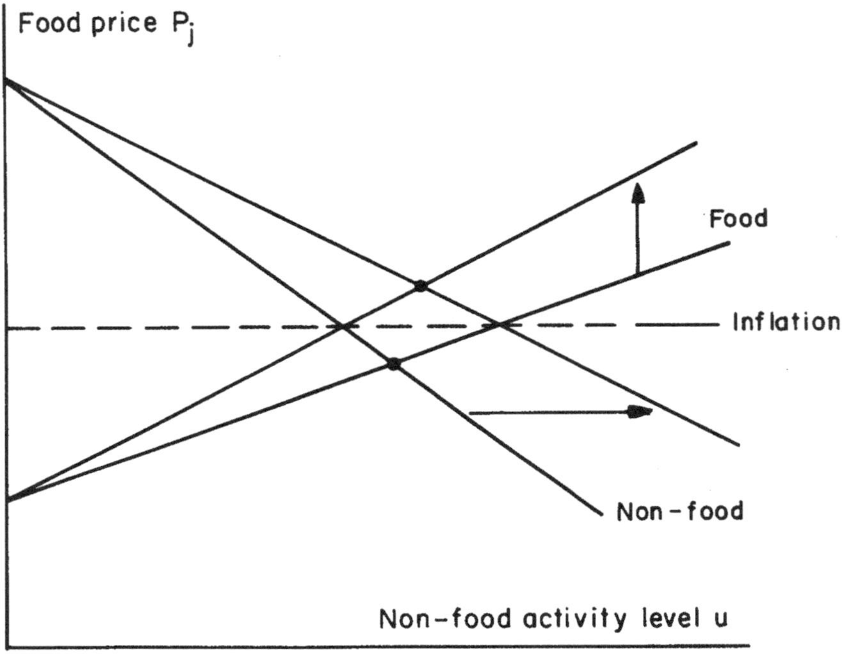

FIGURE 11 Determination of macro equilibrium in markets for food and nonfood. The shifted lines indicate the effects of an attempt to reduce the consumer food price by increasing the subsidy rate applied to the producers' price P_j. The price is driven up, and non-food production can conceivably decline. If the price rises above the inflation line, an agricultural/non-agricultural price spiral may take off.

In (40), a sensible solution requires that the bracketed term multiplying P_j be negative, i.e., food supply exceeds the consumption floor plus demand generated from the sector. When non-food production u rises, some of the extra income is directed toward food. Equation (40) shows that in turn, the food price must rise to stimulate production and cut back on excess demand. This relationship is illustrated by the Food locus in Figure 11.

In the non-food sector, a higher P_j cuts real income and (especially if Engel effects are strong) might lead demand for products from the sector itself to decline. On the other hand, farmers grow richer, and would demand more non-agricultural goods. The non-food locus in Figure 11 can slope either way. Here, we assume the presence of strong Engel effects (realistic in the Third World) so that as P_j rises, u declines.

The shifted lines show what happens when consumers are given a bigger subsidy, or σ is reduced. All household real incomes rise as a consequence, and part of the extra demand goes for non-food commodities. The non-food sehedule rotates to the right. At the same time, the consumer price must rise to cut off the added demand for food that the subsidy generates. Hence, the Food equilibrium locus rotates upward. As Figure 11 shows, the producers' price will rise. Non-food output u might fall, even though the additional food subsidy represents a fiscal expansion.

How sharp will be the producers' price increase? Could P_j go up enough after the reduction in the subsidy parameter to *raise* the consumer price σP_j? The answer evidently depends on the agricultural supply elasticity, say η. Suppose that food is initially not subsidized ($\sigma = 1$) and also that marginal saving rates from both sorts of income are the same, $s_j = \Omega$. Then the consumer price will rise unless the supply elasticity satisfies the condition

$$\eta > \frac{(1-v)(1-\Omega)}{\Omega}.$$

Plausible values for $(1-v)$ and Ω might be 0.3 and 0.15 respectively. In this case, η would have to exceed 1.7 to permit the subsidized food price to fall. The econometric consensus is that even in the long run, an aggregate food supply elasticity of 1.7 is improbably large. The goal of cheaper food seems unattainable via a standard subsidy program unless extra sources of supply are arranged. The obvious possibilities are running down stocks (a short run palliative, at best,) or bringing in imports m_j. With plausible parameters, the elasticity of P_j with respect to m_j might be about −0.5. On the other hand, the elasticity with respect to σ might be 1.5. The implication is that the percentage increase in imports needed to assure a reduction in the consumer food price would have to be larger than the percentage decrease in σ. Import and producer price policies must be integrated in any attempt to increase overall food consumption with a food subsidy program.

In summary, there may well be production limitations to subsidy programs, unless foreign exchange is readily available or the state intervenes actively to shift the food supply curve out by providing inputs to agriculture. On the other hand, food subsidy schemes are politically attractive, and difficult to dismantle once in place. Moreover, they do seem to increase food consumption (with considerable leakage to other commodities) on the part of the poor [46]. Macro policy design when important sectors in the economy cannot be simply aggregated into one is a difficult task. Food provides an important example—the economy is harder to run with subsidies but domestic politics and the lives of the poor are harder without.

Another problem coming from the food markets is their potenital effect on inflation. With food a major proportion of the national consumption basket, agricultural price increases will reduce the real wage and set off inflation in non-agricultural products along the lines of Eq. (6). In terms of Figure 11, an agriculture/non-agriculture price spiral might be set off if P_j rises above the dashed inflation locus. This sort of inflation has been well understood since the early days of the Latin American structuralists—a model was first stated explicitly by Noyola Vasquez [33] following a sketch in Kalecki's lectures in Mexico City the preceding year. The fact that the phenomenon has been recognized for three decades does not make it less important. A shift in the terms of trade toward agriculture is a signal that inflation is soon to follow in most corners of the Third World. Bringing in imports (a costly and administratively difficult process) and trying to shore up agricultural supply comprise the obvious policy response.

4.3. Public enterprise pricing

Not only flexible prices cause fiscal headaches. Setting controlled prices for the products of public enterprises is a major policy issue in many developing countries where the cash flow in entrepreneurial activities of the state may be several times the traditional treasury budget. Private interests cluster around state enterprises because investment of the latter is effective demand for the former. The implications in terms of political economy cannot be overstated, but even standard analytical tools can be used to address the impact on the public deficit of state enterprise activity, as in the innovative computable general equilibrium simulations of Sarker and Panda [35].

Increases in regulated state enterprise prices are frequently viewed as a politically attractive alternative to tighter fiscal policy. Even in countries with a well-established fiscal apparatus, political costs of raising regulated prices may be smaller (or at least levied on different groups) than those of increasing taxes. For countries with large external debts, higher state enterprise prices seem to be the obvious response to the fact that much of the debt is owed directly by such firms. However, depending on the institutional arrangement that regulates financial flows between publicly controlled firms and the treasury, only part of the proceeds from regulated price increases goes to the fiscal accounts; the remainder may finance investment or other outlays. The net effect on aggregate demand cannot be predicted *a priori*—even the net effect on the fiscal deficit is subject to doubt.

All this uncertainty arises because a real increase in regulated prices acts as a cost shock which tends to accelerate inflation, reducing the real value of tax collection. Moreover, high regulated prices may worsen the trade balance because the outputs of state enterprises enter as inputs into tradables. Given the potentially unpleasant economy-wide effects of exchange devaluation, it may make sense to increase the trade surplus by subsidizing regulated prices rather than by increasing them and depreciating the exchange rate. On a similar note, one can ask whether increasing state enterprise prices (typically they produce intermediates) or subsidizing them and increasing the consolidated government deficit is likely to be more inflationary. In a monetarist twist on the model of Eqs. (33) and (34), Sarkar and Panda conclude that in India subsidization will drive up the overall price level by less than overt price increases for the relevant public sector firms.

4.4. Orthodox shocks

We have already observed (Section 3.4) that real interest rates in many developing countries are at an all-time high. Similarly, inflation proceeds apace. One notion that has recently come from Latin America is that both high real interest rates and inertial inflation (in which this period's price increases simply repeat those of last period) might be conquered by a severe wage and price freeze coupled with issuance of a new currency. Arida and

Lara-Resende [2] present the case for a monetary reform such as those enacted in 1985 in Argentina and 1986 in Brazil, while Lopes [26] analyzes the economics of a "heterodox shock" involving inflation control. We take up these ideas in Section 4.5. But before that we should review the unhappy results of orthodox efforts in South America's Southern Cone to reduce inflation in the late 1970's. The new proposals are designed in light of the failures of the old ones.

The keystone of the earlier stabilization package was control of the exchange rate. The practice usually took the form of pre-announcing a slower rate for a crawling peg, to reduce "inflationary expectations," cut pressure on costs and reassure investors. There were effects all over the economy, including financial markets. It makes sense to begin the discussion from the financial angle.

The "other" assets which the exchange rate influences in a system like (38) and (39) are foreign holdings by nationals or claims on the country held abroad. To take a simple case, assume that rentiers hold a quantity Y^* of assets in foreign currency. Bank reserves are R^*, so that total foreign assets of the economy are $J^* = R^* + Y^*$. The total J^* *cannot* change in the short run, since foreign asset stocks only accumulate or decumulate on a flow basis through the current account. If the public reduces its foreign holdings then central bank reserves must rise, and *vice-versa*.

Under these circumstances, the market for domestic deposits will still clear through changes in the interest rate, while quantity adjustment rules for foreign positions. We have a fix/flex system in the financial sphere. It is described by a revised version of our standard model. The equations are

$$\delta\left(i, \hat{P}, \frac{R}{e}, u\right)\left(V + \frac{eJ^*}{F} + 1\right) = \mu\left(1 + \frac{e(J^* - Y^*)}{F}\right) \tag{41}$$

for deposits, and

$$\frac{1}{e}\chi\left(i, \hat{P}, \frac{R}{e}, u\right)\left(V + \frac{eJ^*}{F} + 1\right) = \frac{Y^*}{F} \tag{42}$$

for foreign assets. The adjusting variables are i in (41) and Y^* in (42). Note from the right side of (41) that a reduction in foreign holdings leads to an increase in bank reserves ($R^* = J^* - Y^*$) and consequent monetary expansion. This linkage is the key to under-

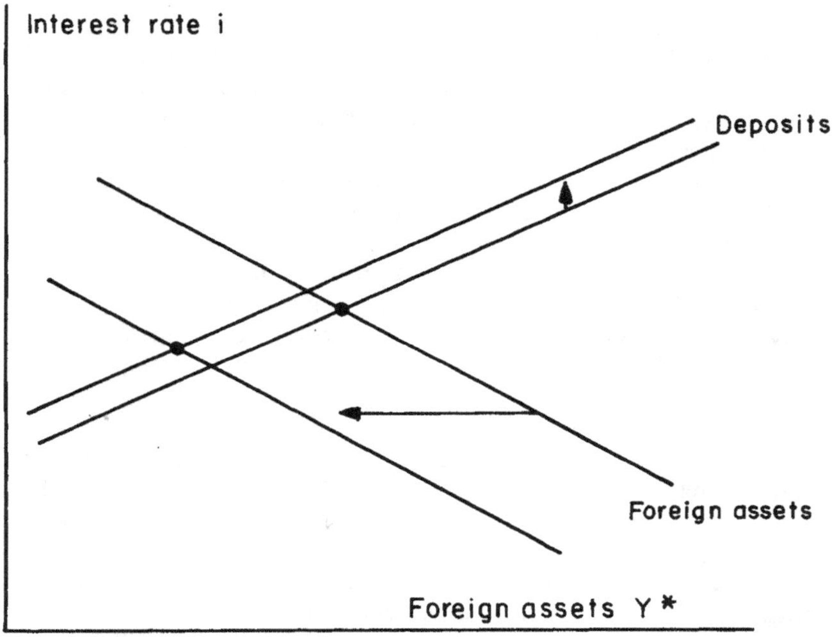

FIGURE 12 Adjustment in asset markets to a fall in the return to holding foreign assets induced by a slower rate of exchange depreciation. A substitution response would tend to increase domestic interest rates. However, bank foreign reserves increase as the public trades in foreign currency, the money supply expands, and interest rates can fall.

standing how the financial system responds to a change in the rate of crawl, as Frenkel [14] and Diaz-Alejandro [11] point out in assessing Southern Cone anti-inflation efforts of the late 1970's. The model here broadly follows Frenkel's.

The story is that the return to holding foreign assets is in part determined by the rate of exchange depreciation in a crawling peg. The relevant comparison is between a return i on domestic assets and $i^* + \hat{e}(=R$ in (41)) on foreign ones. A credible reduction in $\hat{e}$ *reduces* the return to foreign assets and leads to a shift away from Y^*. Domestic interest rates as a consequence go down.

The comparative statics appear in Figure 12. The Deposit schedule slopes upward since a higher Y^* represents a short-term capital outflow. It must be met by a reduction in bank reserves and tighter national credit markets. In the foreign asset market, an increase in i makes holding foreign assets less attractive, and Y^* falls. A fall in R, the return to foreign assets, has two effects. First, the interest rate tends to rise through a substitution effect (the Deposit locus shifts up since the partial derivatives of the demand function δ with respect to i and R are both negative). However, foreign holdings also fall, the money supply rises, and i declines in a leftward shift of the Foreign Asset schedule. The latter adjustment is more important in Figure 12, and probably in practice.

The conclusion is that, other factors being equal, a slower crawl may be associated with reduced interest rates and economic expansion. The "other factors" will of course include the state of confidence in the regime, with political and economic uncertainty leading to capital flight.

Orthodox stabilization packages in the Southern Cone provide an illuminating example. Diaz-Alejandro [11] makes clear that the initial slow-down of the crawling peg brought foreign exchange euphoria to the region. Reducing the return to foreign assets stimulated the domestic economy, making foreign holdings less attractive still. There was positive feedback of the initial reduction of the return to holding foreign assets into itself—a classic symptom of financial instability.

A model is easy to set up in terms of changes in the foreign asset return R and the economy's total foreign assets J^*. Consider how the rates of increase $\dot{R}$ and $\dot{J}^*$ respond to changes in the levels of the two variables:

$\partial\dot{R}/\partial R > 0$: An initial downward jump in R from slowing the crawl increases visible national reserves R^*, cuts interest rates and stimulates growth. National assets look even more attractive and R falls more, making the partial derivative positive.

$\partial\dot{R}/\partial J^* < 0$: Higher foreign assets from any source also make R fall.

$\partial\dot{J}^*/\partial R > 0$: An increase in R pulls the public toward foreign holdings, reducing domestic activity by driving up interest rates and increasing the trade surplus. In this model, (22) should be stated as $e\dot{J}^* = eT + i^*eJ^*$, so that $\dot{J}^*$ rises. The dynamics can be complicated if export lags along the lines of Figure 3 are involved.

$\partial \dot{J}/\partial J^* < 0$: Higher foreign assets lead to more reserves R^* and monetary expansion. The trade balance worsens so that $\dot{J}^* < 0$.

The positive own-derivative $\partial \dot{R}/\partial R$ can underlie a crisis linking the financial and real sides of the economy, along the historical/institutional lines set out by Minsky [31] and Kindleberger [23], and in model form by Taylor and O'Connell [47]. A phase diagram appears in Figure 13, where potential instability is signalled by the fact that R goes up (or down) when it is already above (or below)

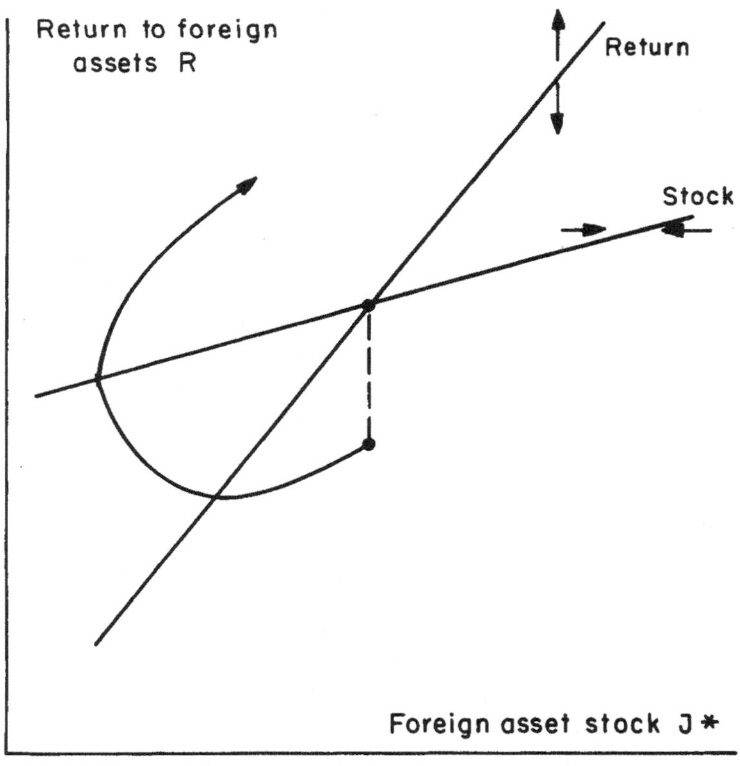

FIGURE 13 Potentially unstable dynamics of the return to foreign assets. An initial downward jump from a slower crawl sets up a process with declining asset stocks from an increased trade gap and (after a period of decrease) a rise in the return. Capital flight, decreased foreign reserves in the banking system, and domestic stagnation are the outcomes.

that Return locus along which $\dot{R}=0$. Slowing a crawling peg makes R jump down from an initial steady state. Foreign assets J^* begin to fall immediately from a reduced trade surplus due to higher activity. However, R continues to decline for a time until the drop in J^* (signalled by a widening trade deficit and over-expansion at home) begins to frighten investors. The return to foreign assets begins to rise as the trajectory crosses the Return schedule. The central bank starts losing reserves, reversing the process in Figure 12. The likely outcome is national economic stagnation before foreign asset stocks start to rebuild through a trade surplus. In practice, the agony is often cut short (or made more acute) by a maxi-devaluation before the trajectory reaches the Stock schedule along which J^* is constant. At that point, speculators are rewarded and currency may start to flow home.

This sad story repeats itself with some frequency in the Third World. There is no certain way to avoid its repetition as long as there are attractive asset markets abroad. However, controls on capital movements can temper destabilizing flows while a sensible crawling peg policy helps keep foreign and domestic asset returns (not to mention profits for exporters or of import substituters) stable relative to each other over time. Steady asset market signals reduce the likelihood of the unstable dynamics of Figure 13. Opening capital markets and dramatically altering returns—the recipe applied by Southern Cone monetarists of the 1970's—may make instability much more likely.

4.5. Heterodox shocks

Besides emphasizing capital controls, policies for stabilization after the debacle of Southern Cone emphasize a more coordinated effort to reduce inflation. Alone with a slower crawl, price and wage control and monetary reform are supposed to combine in a heterodox shock. To trace the likely effects, we have to specify the institutional setting.

The classic structuralist view [Franco, 13] is that extreme inflations are set off by conflicts between internal claims to income and externally imposed restrictions on the trade balance. For example, the hyperinflation of 1922–23 was triggered by Germany's obligations to transfer resources abroad for war reparations and sustained by extensive wage indexation, according to the structuralist account. A heterodox stabilization package gets rid of indexation, and freezes price and wage increases for a time. The question is whether such a program will be viable in its second stage, when controls are lifted and the economy reverts to market-based pricing rules under a foreign resource constraint.

We can look at the possibilities in the framework of this paper by assuming that the economy is externally constrained as in Section 3.2—even after the stabilization it is required to run a substantial trade surplus to meet reparation or debt repayment obligations. For simplicity, assume that there are neither export subsidies nor imports of capital goods. Then, from (17) the level of activity permitted by the trade balance is $\bar{u} = [(\varepsilon/q) - t]/P_0^* a$.

When capacity utilization exceeds $\bar{u}$ there will be inflationary pressure, probably appearing in mark-ups. The simplest way to capture the phenomenon is to suppose that α in (4) is strongly positive, while the target level of capacity use $\bar{u}_\tau$ is set by the external constraint (as just discussed). Also, let deposits *not* be indexed, so that their demand δ decreases with $\hat{P}$ while the inflation tax (scaled by the value of capital stock) becomes $-\hat{P}\delta[1 + (1/V)]$ from the deposit demand function if we ignore external reserves. Plugging these hypotheses in the inflation Eq. (3) and the macro balance relationship (16) gives

$$-\hat{P}\delta\left(1 + \frac{1}{V}\right) + g_0(\tau) - h(i - \hat{P})$$

$$- \Omega\left[\frac{(\varepsilon/q) - t}{P_0^* a} + \frac{1}{\alpha}(\hat{P} - (1 - \phi)\hat{w} - \phi\hat{e})\right] + \gamma + qt = 0$$

Capacity utilization has been eliminated as an adjusting variable by external strangulation, so the inflation rate adjusts to bring internal balance in this equation. A change in $\hat{P}$ has five effects on aggregate demand:

1) A higher $\hat{P}$ increases investment by cutting the real interest rate.

2) It also reduces tax receipts because of collection lags, etc. The overall saving rate Ω falls, or aggregate demand goes up.

3) Faster inflation may stimulate capital flight, forcing the re-

quired trade surplus t up, cutting capacity utilization and making demand pressure rise.

4) Demand goes down as $\hat{P}$ rises because of the inflation tax (if δ has a less than unitary elasticity with respect to $\hat{P}$, as is likely).

5) Demand also declines when $\hat{P}$ accelerates relative to wage inflation w—a forced saving effect.

Offsetting changes are involved. However, as described in Taylor [44] experience with heterodox shocks suggests that cutting the inflation rate *increases* demand—the inflation tax and forced saving effects (4) and (5) dominate. Since a higher interest rate reduces excess demand, $\hat{P}$ and i trade off inversely in holding the level of activity constant, along the Commodity market loci in Figure 14. The slopes will be more shallow as the effect of $\hat{P}$ on the level of activity is stronger.

Without a fully indexed financial system, high inflation drives people from money, reducing the deposit demand function δ. Following the discussion of Section 3.4, bank loan supply will also decline (it fell from 30 to 10 percent of GDP in Argentina as inflation accelerated in the early 1980s). Under such restrictive conditions firms' desired credit is best treated as proportional to activity according to factor $\lambda(i)$. Again ignoring reserves, excess loan demand becomes

$$\lambda(i)u - \xi(i)\delta(i, \hat{P}, u)\left(1 + \frac{1}{V}\right) = 0.$$

Here, faster inflation drives up net credit demand by reducing δ. A higher interest rate cuts back demand by reducing λ and (if deposit and loan rates are linked) increasing δ. At the same time, capital flight may slow, leading the level of activity and credit needs to rise. The implication is that the interest rate effect on excess loan demand is weak, or the loan schedules in Figure 14 have shallow slopes.

Given all this preparation, we can now ask about the effects of policy moves *after* the heterodox shock—there is less indexation, but interest rates and uncontrollable prices are still free to move. How will they respond to perturbation? The upper diagram in Figure 14 shows the effects of more foreign resources, e.g., extra exports or debt foregiveness (or repudiation). The level of activity

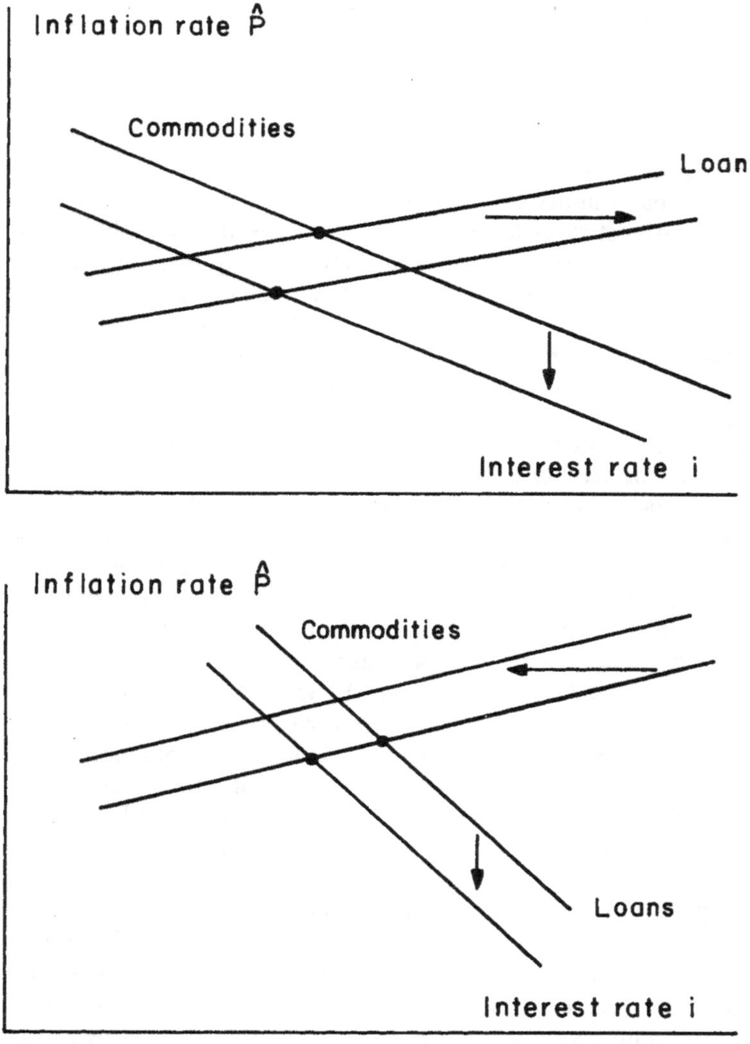

FIGURE 14 The upper diagram shows the effects of extra foreign resources after a heterodox shock. Both the residual inflation and interest rates decline. In the lower diagram, higher fiscal debt placements reduce the interest rate and by increasing the base of the inflation tax slow down *P* as well.

rises, pushing up loan demand and the interest rate. However, inflation drops off as excess demand pressure abates. Given the slopes of the curves, the final results could be falls in *both* inflation and interest rates. The extra dollars help defuse a potentially unstable inflationary situation.

In a somewhat longer time frame, fiscal expansion leading to increased placements of government debt leads the money base to rise and interest rates to decline. At the same time, the base of the inflation tax goes up, reducing the level of $\hat{P}$ required to equilibrate the commodity market. The outcomes again could be lower inflation and interest rates. If the fiscal expenditures go toward projects aimed at generating exports or substituting imports, they can generate foreign exchange and ease inflationary pressures in the medium run.

So far, our conclusions resemble those of Lopes [26]. Unless the initial level of activity is high, a heterodox shock is feasible without contractionary fiscal and monetary policy *if* enough foreign exchange is available to support production and damp excess commodity demand. However, two further considerations must be taken into account. First, flex-price markets can upset the stabilization effort, it there is strong demand pressure in them (perhaps abetted by supply-reducing speculative stock-holding which could be restrained by high interest rates). Second, a visibly restrictive policy may be required to convince external lenders and local rentiers to permit enough capital inflow to hold inflationary pressures down. The contradiction implicit in the shock may be between avoiding depression and responding to orthodox calls for austerity. Just eliminating the inertial component of inflation does not cancel conflicting economic claims or flex-price market bottlenecks. Especially when foreign resources are scarce, continuing frustration of different classes' real income goals can easily provoke a new inflationary burst. The social gain is that the heterodox move reduces the degree of indexation in the system—the new inflation may accelerate less and settle at a lower steady rate than the old.

4.6. Summary about the short run

Our arguments about the short run can be summarized as follows:

1) As is well-known, both devaluation and monetary restriction can easily create stagflation—economic contraction and faster

inflation—in the short run. Medium-term dynamic adjustment of exports and the real wage may combine inflation with stop-go output fluctuations.

2) Both export subsidies and import quotas can be used in lieu of devaluation to avoid some of its unfavorable side-effects. Quota liberalization, in contrast, can easily be stagflationary.

3) Food subsidy schemes can easily drive *up* consumer food prices unless they are coupled with greater imports. Hence, a welfare benefit can only be obtained at a current account cost. This sort of dilemma is characteristic of other sorts of direct fiscal interventions when intersectoral price and quantity interactions are important. A further complication is that a short run increase in food prices can easily trigger an inflationary spiral. This same observation applies to prices of state-controlled enterprises, which often produce key intermediate goods.

4) Financial liberalization in the form of raising interest rates on deposits is stagflationary unless unexpected (but possible) portfolio switches take place. For success, liberalization would have to draw rentiers principally from hedge assets such as "gold" toward productive loans to firms (not bank deposits). Practically speaking, such changes in desired portfolio composition seem unlikely to occur. In any case, many developing countries today face extremely high as opposed to low real interest rates. The heyday of invigorating financial intermediation by increasing bankers' profits has long since passed.

5) A more slowly crawling peg reduces the relative return to holding foreign assets, and may lead to portfolio switches toward domestic assets with a consequent increase in bank reserves. Monetary expansion, stimulating aggregate demand, would occur. With domestic inflation kept up by indexed contracts under conditions of high demand, gradual deterioration of the real exchange rate could lead to current account problems and subsequent capital flight. The policy is counterproductive—as it was in South America's Southern Cone in the late 1970's—unless it is accompanied by policies to reduce domestic inflation. The likelihood of destabilizing speculation against a maxidevaluation can be reduced by a steady crawling peg and controls on capital movements.

6) Wage and price controls in addition to exchange rate control

are being implemented currently in several countries in a policy package called a "heterodox shock." The resulting reductions in inflation and slowing the crawling peg could lead to interest rate reductions and renewed growth. However, the direct effect on aggregate demand is of uncertain sign. If may be negative, due to increased tax collections and reduction of speculative consumption demand. Consumer spending may also rise as the inflation tax is reduced. In the latter case, inflationary outbursts in flex-price markets are a risk. They can be stabilized if imports can be brought in promptly, i.e., if there is available foreign exchange. Ideally, the shock should be administered under conditions of monetary and fiscal ease, but tightness may be required to hold flex-prices steady and reassure suppliers of foreign resources. Fine-tuning both foreign lenders and the domestic impacts of the shock becomes a tricky question.

7) The general conclusion is that at least in the short to medium run, directed policy makes sense. Maneuvers such as quotas and subsidies (or multiple exchange rates) and price controls instead of changes in the exchange rate, monetary, and fiscal policy avoid unfavorable economy-wide side-effects. Administrative skill and appropriate institutional and political conditions are obviously required for directed policy to work; the same is doubly true for coordinated interventions like a heterodox shock. Also, one has to worry about how policies are likely to evolve over time—a topic further addressed in the next chapter.

5. DISTRIBUTION, GROWTH AND INFLATION IN THE MEDIUM RUN

The topic at hand is how inflation and distributional change affect the pattern of growth over time. A full treatment in an open economy model like the one herein could take many pages—Taylor [41] and Marglin and Bhaduri [28] on closed economies are already lengthy. Here, we just point out key linkages, concentrating on the real side of the system. An algebraic treatment is presented for a one-sector model, and extensions to several sectors are briefly sketched.

A few paragraphs should be devoted to setting the stage. The short-run system is described by (6) for inflation, (20) for the interest rate, and equations for internal and external balance. If we don't consider interest rate cost-push, taxes, export subsidies, or government investment, the internal balance relationship is given by an abbreviated version of (18),

$$c_0(\hat{P}) + \gamma + \Theta[g_0(\tau) + h\beta u - h(i - \hat{P})] + \varepsilon - \left[\frac{s\tau}{1+\tau} + \frac{\phi}{1+\tau}\right]u = 0, \tag{43}$$

where the bracketed term multiplying u will be called Ω. The external balance question is (17), where we ignore export subsidy term ζ. Two conditions that are built into (43) fit the capital stock growth rate into the material balance equation for national input,

$$\theta g = \Omega u - c_0 - \gamma - \varepsilon, \tag{44}$$

and relate growth to investment demand,

$$g = g_0 + h\beta u - h(i - \hat{P}). \tag{45}$$

Eliminating u between these two equations gives a reduced form for the growth rate as

$$g = \frac{1}{\Omega - h\beta\Theta}[h\beta(c_0 + \gamma + \varepsilon) + \Omega(g_0 - h(i - \hat{P}))]. \tag{46}$$

There are four variables that evolve over time. Two come from the three input prices: the mark-up rate τ, the real wage z and the real exchange rate q. From (1) and (2) these are related by the price-cost identity

$$1 = (1 + \tau)(zb + qa), \tag{47}$$

so we need only specify differential equations for two of them. For present purposes, it is convenient to discuss evolution of the mark-up rate as in (4),

$$\hat{\tau} = \alpha(u - \bar{u}_\tau), \tag{48}$$

and (using the inflation Eq. (6)) the real exchange rate

$$\hat{q} = \hat{e} - \hat{P} = (1 - \phi)\hat{e} - \frac{\tau\alpha}{1+\tau}(u - \bar{u}_\tau) - (1 - \phi)\psi(u - \bar{u}_w) + (1 - \phi)\lambda(z - \bar{z}). \tag{49}$$

The remaining two state variables are financial: the "velocity" of government debt, $V = P_k K/F$, and the ratio of foreign debt to government debt, $f = F^*/F$. The differential equation for V is

$$\hat{V} = \Theta \frac{P}{P_k} \hat{P} + (1-\Theta) \frac{eP_i^*}{P_k} \hat{e} + g - \frac{P}{P_k} V(\gamma + qt) - i \qquad (50)$$

where we don't consider foreign reserves. Equations (23) and (24) together determine $\hat{f}$.

For all intents and purposes, τ, q, V, and the policy variables γ, μ, and e determine the short-run system. If the economy is not constrained by foreign resources (which is what we assume), the debt ratio f has no direct influence. To recall the main linkages, note from (A.5) that all the variables just listed except μ have positive effects on the interest rate i, inflation rate $\hat{P}$, and real interest rate $i - \hat{P}$ (the latter if deposit demand responds more strongly to inflation than the interest rate, which seems likely.) Inflation and interest rates decline with μ, and rise with capacity utilization u. The direct effects of τ, $\hat{P}$, and q on u are ambiguous—they can be expansionary or contractionary. More fiscal spending γ creates expansion, and a higher real interest rate makes output decline. The trade balance falls with u and g, and improves with a higher value of q.

5.1. Mark-up dynamics

On the basis of this summary, we can consider distributional strife in the long run. In a first exercise, assume that the authorities tie nominal devaluation to the inflation rate. Since $\hat{e}$ is set equal to $\hat{P}$, the real exchange rate is held constant, while the mark-up changes according to (48). Distributional conflict occurs between workers and capitalists, without interaction with the outside world.

In (48) there is no sure presumption as to the sign of α—the mark-up may either rise or (perhaps more likely) fall as output rises. There are two stable cases of dynamic adjustment. Case A has $\alpha > 0$ and a negative system-wide effect of τ on u: $u_\tau < 0$. This sort of output response to income redistribution is sometimes called "stagnationist" since progressive distributional change (away from profits and toward labor) activates a stagnant system. Case B ("exhilarationist") has the opposite signs. If both α and u_τ have the same sign, one has an unstable macro system along the lines of the Harrod growth model.

Case A resembles the monetarist model of Section 2.1, except that output variation is permitted and there is a more coherent distributional story. Consider what happens under expansionary policy—say a permanent increase in the money multiplier μ. From an initial steady state, the real interest rate will fall, stimulating investment demand and capacity utilization. The mark-up will start to rise, and inflation will accelerate from higher capacity use and a worsening real wage. The distributional shift toward profits finally begins to reduce aggregate demand, and u falls back to its steady state level $\bar{u}_{\tau}$. The new steady state ends up with a higher profit share, and faster inflation. From (46) the growth rate can either rise or fall, depending on how strongly τ affects the "animal spirits" term g_0 and the multiplier parameter Ω, and how the consumption intercept term c_0 responds to the inflation rate. If inflation reins in consumption, the growth rate could fall. The steady state real interest rate would rise correspondingly in (45). As discussed in [41], velocity in (50) is usually dynamically stable. As a state variable, it will evolve over time to be consistent with the new interest rate/inflation configuration. Monetary policy matters in the present system, but monetary ratios ultimately adjust to accommodate what happens on the real side.

Case A long run fits orthodox prejudices well. However, it goes against the neoclassical exhilarationist short-run grain, as we will see below. Expansionary policy does not help capacity utilization in the long run, worsens distribution, and can slow growth and raise the real interest rate. Aside from unchanged capacity use, these findings reverse in Case B, where the mark-up rate falls with higher activity but "responsible" capitalists strongly increase investment demand when the mark-up (or the profit share) goes up. One particular prediction from Case B is that expansionary monetary policy first accelerates inflation but then leads it to *fall* in the long run by stimulating producers to cut mark-ups (a godsend that would be enhanced by Cavallo/Patman effects). Empirical evidence on pricing behavior suggests that Case B is plausible, but of course medium term dynamic complications in the inflationary process could make the model's predictions less clearcut. What does come out sharply in both cases is how distributional conflict over time can influence economic change.

5.2. Exchange rate dynamics

A second special model can be built around the real exchange rate, which measures distribution between workers and the rest of the world. We assume that τ stays fixed, or that α is set to zero in (48) and (49). Under this hypothesis, capacity use can vary across steady states. On the other hand, the inflation rate is fixed by the natural (for analytical purposes) assumption that the authorities preset the crawling peg $\hat{e}$, and stick with it. In steady state, $\hat{P}$ must equal $\hat{e}$, though the two inflation rates can differ during transitions.

Stability analysis is based on two processes. First, any increase (or devaluation) of q reduces the real wage z from (47). Inflation accelerates as workers try to regain their real income position, and with a fixed $\hat{e}$, $\hat{q}$ becomes negative. Thus, q returns toward an equilibrium value.

The second process occurs via aggregate demand. If devaluation is expansionary, an increase in q raises u and the inflation rate, and $\hat{q}$ is negative. The signs reverse and are destabilizing if devaluation is contractionary, but the overall adjustment may be stable because of the first process. Instability occurs if $u_q < -(\lambda/\psi)(a/b)$. Strong worker real wage resistance (a large λ) and insensitivity of the inflation rate to the level of activity (small ψ) make stability more likely.

In the stable case, an expansionary move initially stimulates inflation, as usual. There is real exchange appreciation, which carries over to the new steady state. If devaluation is expansionary, the final increase in u is less than that coming from the initial shock; if devaluation is contractionary, the increase is greater. There is leakage from the shock through the current account, but the changes in capacity utilization show it is not complete. The impetus for the change can come from permanent increases in fiscal spending γ, exports ε, or monetary expansion which reduces $i - \hat{P}$. Equation (46) shows that the growth rate goes up in all cases (unless appreciation strongly reduces ε). Export-led growth (or activities that generate foreign resources more generally) fits well into this model. An autonomous increase in ε is expansionary and offsets the current account deterioration resulting from exchange appreciation and a higher activity level. In the model world, export expansion via long-run real devaluation can be induced by speeding up the crawl rate $\hat{e}$. Export and output expansion follow, at the cost of higher inflation and a lower real wage. Growth rate effects are ambiguous.

A final point concerns instability. If devaluation is sufficiently contractionary (even after a lagged adjustment of exports to the exchange rate as in Figure 3), an expansionary shock sets off an inflationary spiral. Exchange appreciation from an initial burst of inflation leads to a further rise in output, additional inflation and appreciation, and so on. A maxi-jump in the nominal exchange rate may break the spiral, but only for a time. Such a story is not far-fetched in some contexts.

5.3. Long-run distribution among all concerned

When both the mark-up and exchange rate can vary, there is potential conflict among all parties. However, labor is protected by a balance of forces. Our "natural rate" hypothesis about the mark-up is that it is stable at the activity level $\bar{u}_\tau$. From the side of costs, steady state inflation will settle at the rate $\hat{e}$ of devaluation. Plugging these conditions into (7) and setting $\hat{z}=0$ gives

$$z=\frac{\psi(\bar{u}_\tau-\bar{u}_w)-\hat{e}}{\lambda}+\bar{z} \tag{51}$$

so that z falls in steady state when $\hat{e}$ is stepped up, but is stable otherwise.

The implication is that τ and q will do the adjusting to demand shocks across steady states, at given capacity utilization. They are tied together by (47), so if one rises the other falls. Across steady states, when these variables change i will adjust in (43) to clear the commodity market. Under appropriate stability conditions (not explored here) V will evolve to bring portfolio equilibrium in (20). The trade balance adjusts in (17) and foreign debt is an accommodating state variable. Hence we have a well-determined system.

To explore stability, we need only analyze one of the differential equations for τ and q, subject to (47) and (51). If we work with (48), it is easy to see from (47) that the overall stability condition is

$$\alpha\left[u_\tau-\frac{1}{a(1+\tau^2)}u_q\right]<0. \tag{52}$$

This equation gives rise to six cases of stable adjustment, depending on the signs of α and the system-wise response parameters u_τ and u_q. Our Cases A and B on the sign of α (positive and negative respectively) are crossed with both expansionary and contractionary effects of τ and q on the level of capacity utilization.

Consider Case B. With $\alpha < 0$, the term in brackets in (52) must be positive. That can happen with $u_\tau > 0$ (the stability condition in the model with q fixed) when there is contractionary devaluation or else u_q is not too strongly positive. Contractionary devaluation can also be coupled with $u_\tau < 0$, making a third case. Similar combinations of output responses with $\alpha > 0$ give rise to the six cases.

As before, we consider two kinds of shocks—an output expansion stimulated by fiscal or monetary policy or increased exports, and a more rapidly crawling nominal exchange rate. It is easy to show that the sign of α determines what happens to the mark-up rate when there is expansion—τ falls when $\alpha < 0$ and rises when $\alpha > 0$. Subject to (47), q moves the other way. In the "monetarist" version with α positive, expansionary policy leads not only to a worse income distribution and inflation, but to real appreciation and export deterioration as well. These outcomes reverse when $\alpha < 0$.

The signs of responses of the mark-up and real exchange rate to a faster crawl in the six stable cases are as follows:

	Case	Responses of	
	$\alpha > 0$	q	τ
A.1	$u_q > 0,\ u_\tau < 0$	+	+
A.2	$u_q > 0,\ u_\tau > 0$	−	+
A.3	$u_q < 0,\ u_\tau < 0$	+	−
	$\alpha < 0$		
B.1	$u_q > 0,\ u_\tau > 0$	+	−
B.2	$u_q < 0,\ u_\tau < 0$	−	+
B.3	$u_q < 0,\ u_\tau > 0$	+	+

In the "odd" cases A.2 and B.2 where an adjustment based on τ alone would be unstable, a faster crawl causes real *appreciation* because the mark-up rate rises sharply. When $\alpha < 0$, for example, an increase in $\hat{e}$ leads q initially to rise from (49). The effect is to reduce capacity utilization when devaluation is contractionary, so that τ starts to rise. The real wage is reduced by both developments, and inflation speeds up. If the price acceleration is fast enough the real exchange rate is eroded, and the system arrives at a new inflationary equilibrium where the attempt at devaluation has failed. Real appreciation and a higher mark-up offset each other in restoring u to its equilibrium level $\bar{u}_\tau$.

5.4. Economic regimes

The foregoing discussion shows that when output is the macroeconomic adjustment variable, then income redistribution and growth interact in surprising fashion. The usual neoclassical view is that real wage reductions should make output rise in the short run. Here, such a response occurs in Case B because of strong investment demand. A higher profit share stimulates enterpreneurs' animal spirits, they push up capital formation, and output follows. However, neoclassical substitutional responses point in the same direction. Lower wages should stimulate employment and lead output to increase from the side of supply. The irony is that this exhilarationist story is associated with non-orthodox responses to expansionary policy in the long run, while the stagnationist Case A gives orthodox results.

We can also ask about the effects of upper bounds on capacity utilization u, say from foreign exchange (as in Section 4.5), short harvests, or full use of available capital stock. In so doing, a useful first step is to derive the distribution/output relationship explicitly in a stripped-down version of the basic model. From the saving side, output growth g^S is determined by

$$g^S = sr - \gamma = s\pi u - \gamma \qquad (53)$$

where we define π as the share of profits in output. It is easy to verify that π is an increasing function of the mark-up rate: $\pi = \tau/(1+\tau)$. We don't consider imports of capital stock in a closed economy model, and one can easily show that $r = u\tau/(t+\tau)$ by playing with identities.

In Eq. (12), investment demand g^I is treated as a function of τ (or π) and r. However, in light of the above identities, it can just as well be related to π and u. We follow that specification here.

Excess aggregate demand is $g^I - g^S$. It must equal zero for macroeconomic equilibrium, and the short-run stability condition (if capacity utilization adjusts to drive excess demand to zero) is that investment demand respond less strongly than saving to higher capacity, or $g_u^I - g_u^S < 0$. An increase in γ will raise u for a given π, while the derivative of capacity utilization with respect to the profit share is

$$\frac{du}{d\pi} = \frac{-(g_\pi^I - g_\pi^S)}{g_u^I - g_u^S}. \tag{54}$$

The denominator in (54) is negative from the short-run stability condition. Hence, the sign of the derivative depends on $g_\pi^I - g_\pi^S$. If a higher profit share does not stimulate much extra investment when π itself is low, the sign of $du/d\pi$ can switch from negative to positive as π rises over some range. The relationship is sketched in Figure 15, following Marglin and Bhaduri [28]. If we assume that short-run macro adjustment occurs rapidly, the economy will always be at some point on the "Commodity market" locus. Capacity utilization u is a function of the profit share π and fiscal expenditure γ, and an increase in γ shifts the locus to the right.

Note that along the upper branch of the locus, an increase in π leads u to decline—this is the stagnationist Case A of Section 5.1. Along the lower branch—Case B—a rising profit share increases capacity utilization via investment demand. The position and curvature of the Commodity market locus reflect a supposition that stagnationist responses are more likely when real wages are low or profits high. With high real wages (a low π) investment demand and substitution effects may dominate, leading to an exhilarationist system. Other configurations of the curve (e.g. convex instead of concave from the left) are of course possible.

What happens if there is an upper bound on capacity utilization, at level $\bar{u}$? Figure 16 illustrates the possibilities. In the short run, the available macro equilibrium positions lie along the solid locus. As successively lower levels of the profit share, there is a stagnationist Section A, full capacity use at u, and then an exhilarationist stretch B. The small arrows show the mode of adjustment. Capacity use changes along segments A and B. Along segment C, incipient excess demand leads prices to rise, the profit share to to up, and output to fall back toward the full capacity level. Along the exhilarationist Section D, higher profits cause initial excess demand to *rise,* leading to further disequilibrium—the economy is unstable.

The equilibrium point can arrive at segments C and D for several

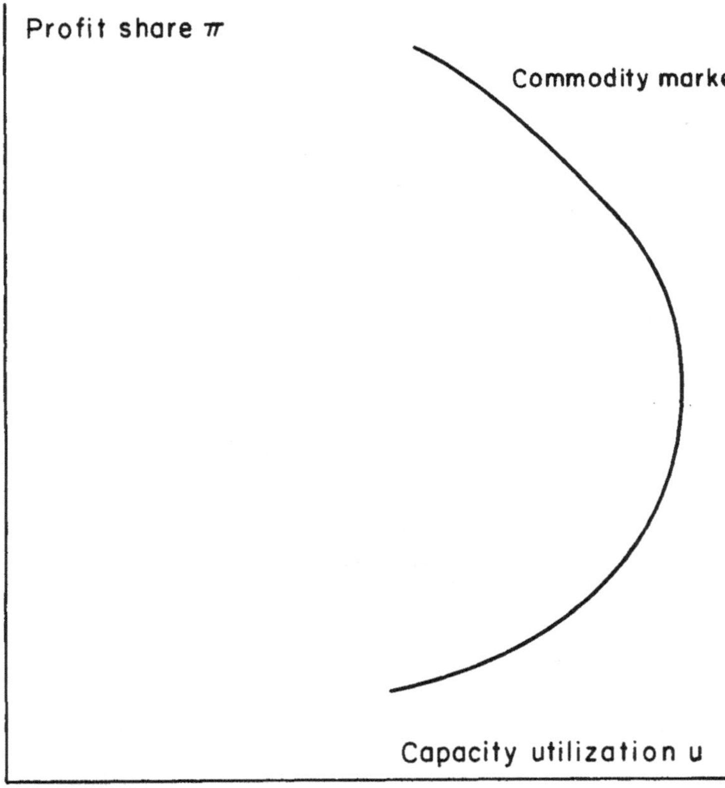

FIGURE 15 The relationship between income distribution and output in the short run. Capacity utilization adjusts rapidly so that the equilibrium always lies along the Commodity market locus. Income redistribution toward wages or away from profits leads output to increase along the upper (Case A or stagnationist) branch. Progressive redistribution makes output fall along the lower (Case B or exhilarationist) segment of the curve.

reasons, e.g. an adverse supply shock reducing $\bar{u}$, expansionary policy which increases u for a given value of π, or progressive income redistribution in a stagnationist system. What the diagram illustrates is that such changes can radically affect the way the economy behaves by altering distributional trade-offs.

This point can be made in various ways. One would be through making α and u_τ in Section 4.1 functions of u and π. Sign changes

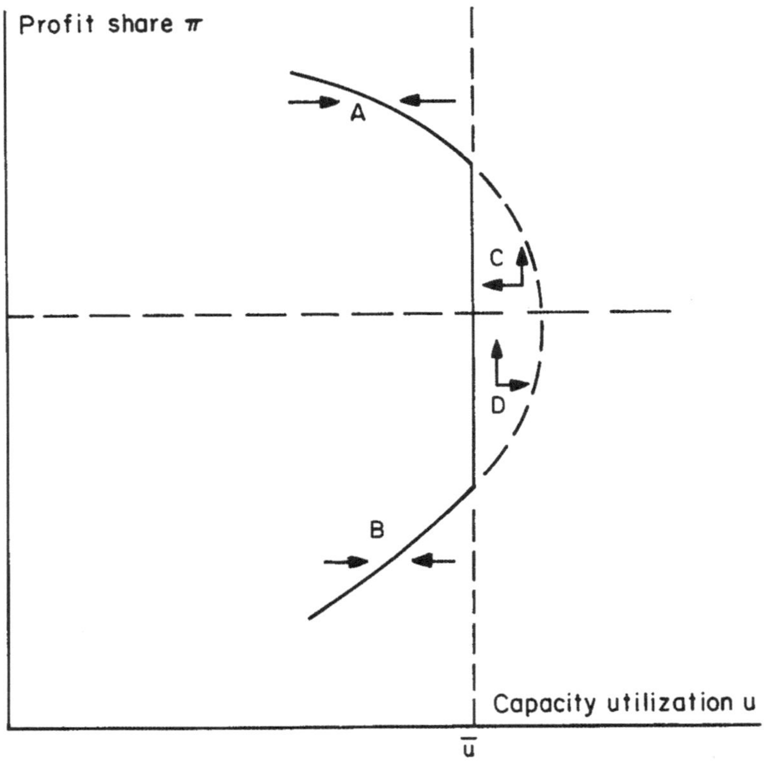

FIGURE 16 Macroeconomic adjustment regimes. The economy has potential equilibrium positions along the solid curves. Below the capacity upper bound $\bar{u}$ output is the adjusting variable, and income redistrubiton is stagnationist and exhilarationist in regions A and B respectively. Stable forced saving/inflation tax adjustment occurs in region C. Instability arises in region D, with faster inflation exacerbating excess commodity demand.

would delineate the various regimes. Alternatively, regimes changes are recognized in recent disequilibrium macroeconomics, e.g. Benassy [5] refers to segments A, B, and C respectively as "Keynesian," "classical," and "repressed inflation" regimes. However, this literature does not fully develop the distributional and inflationary implications of changes in the mode of macro adjustment.

Empirical assessments summarized in Taylor [44] point in the direction of stagnationist responses in many developing countries. Hence, expansionary policy or progressive income redistribution runs some risk of inducing adjustment via forced saving and the inflation tax. If output bounds are not reached, long-run adjustment will be orthodox, unless the economy shifts toward an exhilarationist short-run adjustment mode.

5.5. Extensions to several sectors

The model of this chapter can be extended naturally to several sectors. For simplicity, we maintain the assumption that output is the adjusting variable in each sector (upper bounds on output are not reached). We also suppose that a sector's capital stock once installed cannot shift. Short run demand conditions will then determine differing rates of profit across sectors, whether their outputs adjust under a mark-up pricing rule, or their outputs are fixed and prices clear the market (as in the Dutch disease and flexible food price models discussed in Sections 3.3 and 4.2, respectively). Investment demands by sector will respond to profit rates and/or levels of capacity utilization—low (high) profits will stimulate slow (fast) capacity growth and cross-sectoral effects of profits on investment can be taken into account.

Following Taylor [42], an illustrative two-sector model of this type focusing on the potential effects of redistributive policies is easy to construct. It is based on a w-sector producing wage goods and a p-sector making capital goods and commodities consumed by both income classes. For simplicity, mark-up pricing is assumed to apply in both sectors; prices are normalized to equal one. The saving-investment balance (in intensive form) is

$$\lambda g_w + g_p - s(\lambda r_w + r_p) = 0 \tag{56}$$

where the g_i are growth rates of capital stocks (assumed non-shiftable between sectors once installed), the r_i are profit rates, s is the saving rate from profits, and $\lambda = K_w/K_p$ is the ratio of capital stocks by sector.

Let α now stand for the marginal propensity to consume w-sector products from wage income, and Θ be a shift term toward demand for goods from that sector. The shift is reckoned proportional to the economy-wide total capital stock, and could represent Engel effects, income redistribution via taxes or subsidies toward wage-earners, etc. Demand supply equilibrium for the w-sector can be shown to take the form

$$-\frac{\beta\lambda}{\tau_w} r_w + \frac{\alpha}{\tau_p} r_p + \Theta(\lambda + 1) = 0 \tag{57}$$

where the τ_i are sectoral mark-up rates and $\beta = (1 + \tau_w - \alpha) > 0$.

The saving-investment balance (56) and the commodity material balance Eq. (57) form a convenient system for determining the profit rates r_w and r_p (and implicitly sectoral output levels, the income distribution, etc.). Note that the two profit rates trade off inversely at given levels of saving. A rise in one rate would generate excess saving that would have to be offset in equilibrium through a fall in the other rate. This relationship is shown by the negatively sloped "Saving" line in Figure 17.

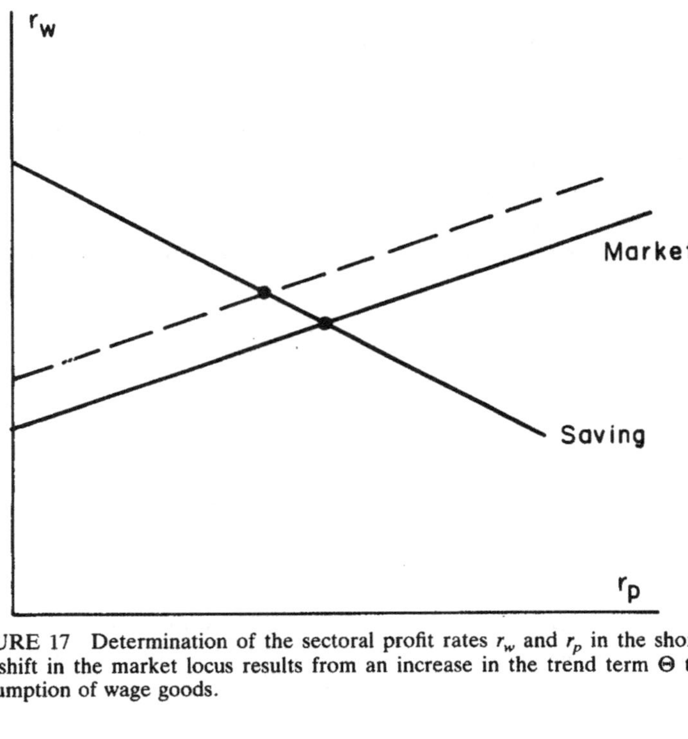

FIGURE 17 Determination of the sectoral profit rates r_w and r_p in the short run. The shift in the market locus results from an increase in the trend term Θ toward consumption of wage goods.

In the market for w-goods, an increase in r_w is associated with excess supply—the marginal propensity to consume wage goods from the income generated by an increase in output X_w is less than one. An increase in r_p raises demand. Hence, to hold excess demand to zero, r_w and r_p trade off along the positively sloped "Market" line in Figure 17—a rise in r_p calls forth an increase in supply (associated with a higher r_w) to restore equilibrium.

Various comparative static exercises can be carried out in this frame-work—we mention the major one. An increase in autonomous demand for wage goods (a higher Θ) represents redistributive policy. The result is an upward shift of the market locus, leading to a higher r_w (and X_w) and lower r_p (and X_p). These shifts do *not* unambiguously affect growth rates and income distribution. To see why we have to bring more analytical apparatus to play.

First note that if we define a determinant Δ as

$$\Delta = \frac{\tau_p}{\alpha}\frac{\beta}{\tau_w} = \frac{\tau_p}{\alpha}\frac{(1+\tau_w-\alpha)}{\tau_w}, \tag{58}$$

then explicit solutions for the profit rates are:

$$r_w = \frac{1}{(1+\Delta)\lambda}\left[\frac{\lambda g_w + g_p}{s} + \frac{\tau_p(1+\lambda)}{\alpha}\Theta\right] \tag{59}$$

and

$$r_p = \frac{1}{(1+\Delta)}\left[\frac{\Delta(\lambda g_w + g_p)}{s} - \frac{\tau_p(1+\lambda)}{\alpha}\right]. \tag{60}$$

In a system with excess capacity, growth itself depends on investment demand. In each sector, entrepreneurs' desired growth g_i can be assumed to be a function of the profit rate r_i and capacity utilization (X_i/K_i) as a proxy for an accelerator term. But as we saw in connection with Eq. (11), rates of capacity utilization can be uniquely related to profit rates, so the investment demand functions become:

$$g_i = g_0 + \phi_i r_i, \qquad i = w \quad \text{or} \quad p. \tag{61}$$

The term g_0 here is autonomous demand for investment, assumed for simplicity to be the same in the two sectors. Its level may depend on institutional factors, population growth, and technological change. The response terms ϕ_w and ϕ_p can differ—a more "dynamic" or "entrepreneurial" sector might be expected to have a higher coefficient.

Since r_w and r_p are given by (59) and (60), one can use (61) to solve for the growth rates as:

$$g_w = \frac{1}{\Gamma}\left\{g_0\left[1 + \frac{1}{(1+\Delta)s}\left(\frac{\phi_w}{\lambda} - \phi_p\Delta\right)\right] + \frac{\phi_w}{\lambda(1+\Delta)}\left(1 - \frac{\phi_p}{s}\right)(1+\lambda)\bar{\Theta}\right\} \quad (62)$$

and

$$g_p = \frac{\phi_1}{\Gamma}\left\{g_0\left[1 - \frac{\lambda}{(1+\Delta)s}\left(\frac{\phi_w}{\lambda} - \phi_p\Delta\right)\right] - \frac{\phi_p}{1+\Delta}\left(1 - \frac{\phi_w}{s}\right)(1+\lambda)\bar{\Theta}\right\} \quad (63)$$

where $\bar{\Theta} = (\tau_p/\alpha)\Theta$.

In these expressions, Γ is another determinant:

$$\Gamma = 1 - \left[\frac{\Delta\phi_p}{(1+\Delta)s} + \frac{\phi_w}{(1+\Delta)s}\right]. \quad (64)$$

The usual expectation is that Γ should be positive, for reasons given below.

We can now ask what happens to the income distribution in the short run when the demand trend parameter Θ changes. Let asterisks denote wage and non-wage income flows divided by the p-sector capital stock.

$$Y_w^* = \frac{Y_s}{P_p K_p} = \frac{r_w}{\tau_w}\lambda + \frac{r_p}{\tau_p}$$

and

$$Y_p^* = \frac{Y_p}{P_p K_p} = r_w\lambda + r_p$$

A natural measure of inequality is ω, the ratio of wage to non-wage income:

$$\omega = \frac{Y_w}{Y_p} = \frac{Y_w^*}{Y_p^*} = \frac{(r_w/\tau_w)\lambda + (r_p/\tau_p)}{r_w\lambda + r_p}$$

The economics of distributional shifts is straightforward. On the assumptions of the model Y_w and Y_p represent labor and non-labor content of total output. Assume for a moment that there is no effect of profit rates on investment or growth rates. In two-factor/two-commodity models of international trade, an increase in one factor will raise the production of the commodity intensive in its use, and lower production of the other commodity. The converse is also true, that if demand for one good rises and the other one falls, then if the good with rising demand is more labor intensive, the total labor content of output will go up.

An increase in Θ shifts the composition of demand in the present model toward wage goods. The labor-output ratios in the two sectors are b_w and b_p. From mark-up equations like (1) and (2) with price levels normalized at unity, it is easy to see that if wage goods are labor intensive with $b_w > b_p$, then $\tau_p > \tau_w$. This criterion enters into the formal expression for $d\omega/d\Theta$, which also takes account of the feedback of the profit rates r_i into growth rates g. The ratio of wage to non-wage income will rise with Θ when the following condition is satisfied:

$$(\tau_p - \tau_w)\left[r_p\left(1 - \frac{\phi_p}{s}\right) + \lambda r_w\left(1 - \frac{\phi_w}{s}\right)\right] > 0. \tag{65}$$

The following observations are immediate:

1) If the bracketed term on the left of (65) is positive, a demand shift toward wage goods will shift the distribution toward wages when $\tau_p > \tau_w$ or wage goods are a low productivity sector. If this intensity condition is reversed, an income transfer toward wage earners will shift the distribution toward profits, presumably not the desired result.

2) At the level of aggregation used here, it is by no means obvious empirically that $b_w > b_p$. The message of many input-output demand composition studies undertaken the past two decades is that the consumption basket of the well-to-do may be quite labor intensive—in high tech services like medical care in rich countries and in domestic servants in poor ones. A serious empirical question arises about the likely impact of redistributive policies.

3) The effect of a shift in Θ is attenuated insofar as the investment response coefficients ϕ_p and ϕ_w approach the saving rate. Suppose that in the dynamic p-goods sector ϕ_p even exceeds s—a rise in the profit rate stimulates more investment demand than

it raises saving. If ϕ_p is big enough to make the bracketed expression in (65) negative, then a shift in demand *away* from p-goods as Θ rises would depress the economy but release labor for wage goods production if the p-sector were labor intensive. The income distribution would shift toward wages but stagnation would result. This outcome resembles the Latin American structuralist story mentioned below.

The next step is to extend this analysis to the long run, conventionally represented by a steady state. A modest amount of additional work is required, as follows.

The system will be in steady state when g_w and g_p—the sectoral capital stock growth rates—are equal. Since $\lambda = K_w/K_p$, it (and other variables such as profit rates, the ratio of wage to non-wage income, etc.) will be constant at steady state. The growth rate of λ is $\lambda = g_w - g_p$. Using (62) and (63), one can show that λ evolves over time according to the equation

$$\dot{\lambda} = \frac{\lambda(1+\lambda)}{\Gamma(1+\Delta)} \left\{ \frac{g_0}{s}\left(\frac{\phi_w}{\lambda} - \phi_p \Delta\right) + \left[\frac{\phi_w}{\lambda}\left(1 - \frac{\phi_p}{s}\right) + \phi_p\left(1 - \frac{\phi_w}{s}\right)\right]\tilde{\Theta} \right\} \tag{66}$$

The interesting steady state occurs when the term in curly brackets is zero. So long as Θ is not excessively negative (for $\phi_p < s$) or positive (for $\phi_p > s$) the derivative of the bracketed term with respect to λ is negative. Hence, for $\Gamma > 0$, the economy will approach steady state.

From (64) the condition that $\Gamma > 0$ is equivalent to:

$$s > \frac{\Delta \phi_p}{1+\Delta} + \frac{\phi_w}{1+\Delta}, \tag{67}$$

or the saving rate from profits must exceed a weighted average of sectoral investment demand responses to a higher profit rate. If the inequality is violated because of overly sensitive investment demand, then the economy will be unstable around its "warranted" steady growth path, along the lines suggested by Harrod long ago.

Note from (62) and (63) that when $\Gamma > 0$, g_w decreases as a function of λ, while g_p goes up. Relatively more capital in place in the w-sector reduces the profit rate there, and thus the sector's investment demand. At the same time, the p-sector's profit and

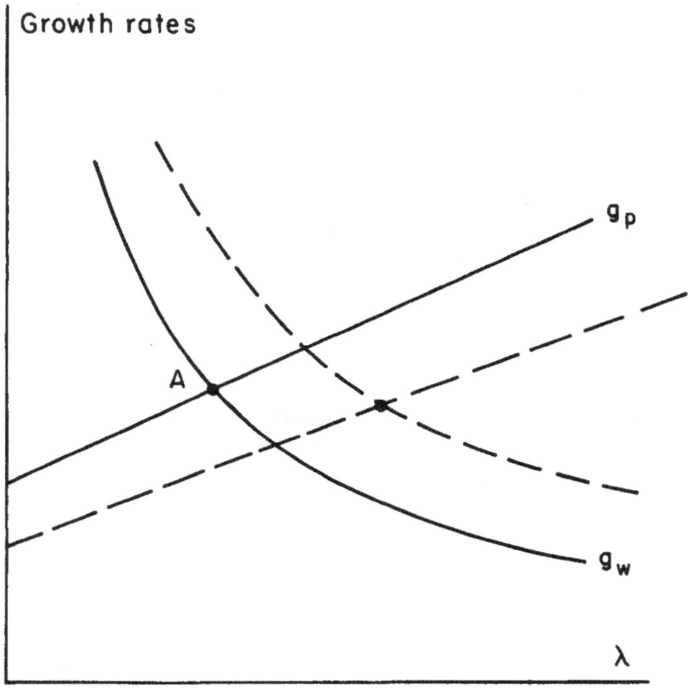

FIGURE 18 Determination of steady state values of the growth rate g and sectoral capital stock ratio λ. An initial equilibrium is A, and the dashed lines represent the effect of an increase in trend consumption toward wage goods.

investment rates rise. Figure 18 gives a graphical representation, with the steady state determined at a point A where the loci for g_w and g_p intersect. An increase in Θ raises g_w for a given λ, again by shifting the profit rate. By a similar mechanism, g_p declines. The outcome (dashed lines) is a rise in the steady state capital stock ratio λ, but an ambiguous shift in the rate of growth.

In one extreme case, if investment in wage goods is lethargic and ϕ_w close to zero, then the dominant shift will be in the g_p schedule, and the steady growth rate will fall. Redistribution towards wages in this case would slow growth in the long run. If ϕ_p is near zero while ϕ_w is relatively large, the opposite result of faster growth would occur. The sign of the effect of an increase in Θ depends only on the investment parameters, as the algebraic solutions for steady state values of g and λ reveal:

$$g = \frac{1}{\Gamma}\left\{g_0 - \left[\frac{\phi_p - \phi_w}{1+\Delta}\right]\tilde{\Theta}\right\} \tag{68}$$

and

$$\lambda = \frac{\phi_w\left[\frac{g_0}{s} + \left(1 - \frac{\phi_p}{s}\right)\tilde{\Theta}\right]}{\phi_p\left[\frac{g_0\Delta}{s} - \left(1 - \frac{\phi_w}{s}\right)\tilde{\Theta}\right]} \tag{69}$$

If Θ (or $\tilde{\Theta}$) is less than zero, so that there is a secular shift in spending away from wage goods by workers, then growth will be fast when $\phi_p > \phi_w$. Dynamic investment response and consumption trends interact synergistically in this case. The result would be stronger if investment demand itself responds to technical change. More rapid technical advance could foster scrapping and make Θ negative. At the same time, g_0 (or separate sectoral analogs) might rise. In that case, growth would be doubly accelerated. A further cumulative effect could come from stimulation of technical progress by growth, as in the "Verdoorn's Law" of Kaldor [20].

The last two questions have to do with possible equalization of profit rates in the long run and steady state redistributional effects. Even though sectoral growth rates are equal in steady states, the same need not be true of profit rates, as can be seen directly from the investment demand functions (61). Only if the response parameters ϕ_i are equal will profit rates equalize. Uniformly responsive investors across the whole economy may or may not be a plausible long run hypothesis. Negative values of trend demand for most "old" sectors and positive values for a few "new" ones are likely in a multi-sectoral system. The natural offset would be differential investment parameters by sector, even though the whole economy might be tending toward steady state.

The final issue is the effect of changes in Θ on the steady state income distribution. When $g_w = g_p = g$, the ratio ω of wage to non-wage income becomes:

$$\omega = \frac{\tau_p + \tau_w\Delta}{\tau_w\tau_p(1+\Delta)} + (\tau_p - \tau_w)s(\tilde{\Theta}/g) \tag{70}$$

As in the short run, a change in Θ affects distribution directly through the factor-intensity term $\tau_p - \tau_w$. However, Θ also influences the steady state growth rate g from (68), and a change in g should alter the income distribution by shifting the saving supply required to meet investment demand.

Remarkably, differentiation of (70) and substitution from (68) show that this latter effect washes out around a stable steady state. The algebraic reason is that g in (68) is a linear function of $\tilde{\Theta}$, so that in the ratio $\tilde{\Theta}/g$ in (70), the growth rate derivative cancels out. More generally, factor-intensity considerations will determine distributional response so long as growth is not dramatically affected by changes in Θ. In (70), with long-run stability ($\Gamma > 0$), the long run wage share rises with Θ when $\tau_p > \tau_w$ or wage goods are the low productivity sector. But from (68) the distributional improvement comes at the cost of slower growth, if the p-sector has the more dynamic investment response. A demand trend away from wage goods helps both distribution and growth when p-goods are labor intensive.

These results all depend on the demand-driven causality in the model which is consistent with the long literature in economics on interactions between demand composition and relative stagnation. The precursors date at least as far back as the reformer Sismondi in post-Napoleonic France [Lustig, 27]. He thought that redistribution toward workers would stimulate demand for industrial products like textiles.

Contemporary outcomes may not prove so desirable. The wealthy may prefer services and sophisticated manufactures, for example, and poor people simple industrial products and food. If investment by sector responds to demand changes, then redistribution can move the economy to a new steady state. The outcomes need not be heartening for proponents of redistributional policy. If profit income recipients preferentially consume labor-intensive services, then on the basis of standard factor-intensity considerations a tax-*cum*-transfer aimed at shifting the distribution toward labor will reduce the wage share in a two-sector system. Moreover, if investors respond strongly to demands for commodities preferred by rentiers, we have just seen that overall growth and capacity utilization can decline.

Latin American structuralists like Tavares [39] and Furtado [15] more or less viewed the world along such lines, but with causality reversed. If industrialization beyond production of simple goods like food and textiles is to occur, they said, then income concentration to sustain demand for more sophisticated commodities (especially those with production technology subject to economies of scale) is unavoidable under present social conditions. Taylor and Bacha [45] provide a formalization. Investment responds to increased consumer demand for "luxuries," leading to forced saving in a full capacity use specification. The distributional shift stimulates luxury sales, and further investment growth. The economy goes through a transition between steady states without and with luxury goods production.

Indian debate follows Sismondi more closely, though with emphasis on the role of public capital formation and the state enterprises. Demand composition may indeed underlie slow industrial growth, e.g., Dutt [12] and Nayyar [32]. Chakravarty [8] further cautions like the Latins that unless steps are taken to preclude regressive distributional shifts, more rapid growth may benefit only the top segment of the income spectrum. A counter-argument is that stagnation may result from limited capacity in infrastructure. The situation is said to be exacerbated by inefficient public enterprise and bureaucratic meddling which dampens private sector animal spirits.

Attempts at empirical analysis of this complex of ideas have been incomplete at best. Studies based on consumer expenditure surveys coupled with input-output tables have found no great variation in *marginal* propensities to consume by sector—the relevant parameters—across income classes. Computations thus showed that income redistribution would not change sectoral output composition very much. Directions of effects also varied across economies. As we have already noted, in some cases redistribution toward the rich would stimulate employment via the service sectors; in others not.

The major problem with this work is that it did not consider feedbacks of changes in demand to investment and productivity gains—this is a promising area of research. Also, more explicit policy considerations can be built in. One example is incorporation of tariffs and subsidies in the determination of sectoral profit rates and therefore investment demand and growth. Using models like the present one augmented with commercial policy tools, Buffie [6] and Taylor [43] show that currently modish "equal incentives" trade policies need not maximize overall output growth in investment-driven models.

A final note is that studies along these lines can only make sense when they take account of the institutional context. For example, Sylos-Labini [38] attributes the 1929 stock market crash to speculation stemming from income concentration in the U.S. in the 1920s. Concentration occurred for institutional reasons—public agencies created to supervise price ceilings instead maintained floors at the same time as real labor incomes fell due to rapid productivity increase. And of course, Wall Street is a particularly American institution. Similarly imaginative interpretations of events in developing countries have yet to appear.

5.6. Summary about the long run

From the Kaleckian perspective of the models of this chapter, it is clear that distributional tensions among workers, capitalists and foreigners strongly affect long run patterns of economic growth. The examples presented here are not meant to be descriptive; rather, they should raise awareness that distributional forces matter. Just *how* they matter is a topic that can only be explored in terms of a model of class structure and conflict that is appropriate for a given economy. But both the long and short run results show that orthodox policy proposals are based on particular closures and further hypotheses about which sorts of interventions are acceptable and which are not. The orthodox code is not a canon that applies at all places and times. The models presented here were designed to show instances in which it breaks down. There are no doubt many others which spring from the institutions of economies in the Third World.

References

[1] Amadeo, Edward "Keynes's Principle of Effective Demand and its Relationship to Alternative Theories of Distribution and Accumulation," Department of Economics, Harvard University, Unpublished Ph.D. dissertation, 1985.

[2] Arida, Persio, and Andre Lara-Resende "Inertial Inflation and Monetary Reform in Brazil," in John Williamson (ed.) *Inflation and Indexation: Argentina, Brazil, and Israel,* Institute of International Economics, 1985.

[2a] Arndt, H. W., "The Origins of Structuralism," *World Development,* **13**: 151–159, 1985.

[3] Bacha, Edmar L. "Growth with Limited Supplies of Foreign Exchange: A Reappraisal of the Two-Gap Model," in Moshe Syrquin, Lance Taylor, and Larry Westphal (eds.) *Economic Structure and Performance*: *Essays in Honor of Hollis B. Chenery,* Academic Press, 1984.

[4] Barbone, Luca "Essays on Trade and Macro Policy in Developing Countries," Department of Economics, Massachusetts Institute of Technology, Unpublished Ph.D. dissertation, 1985.

[5] Benassy, Jean-Pascal *The Economics of Market Disequilibrium,* Academic Press, 1982.

[6] Buffie, Edward "Commercial Policy, Growth, and the Distribution of Income in a Dynamic Trade Model," Department of Economics, University of Pennsylvania, 1986.

[7] Cavallo, Domingo "Stagflationary Effects of Monetarist Stabilization Policies," Department of Economics, Harvard University, Unpublished Ph.D. dissertation 1977.

[8] Chakravarty, Sukhamoy "India's Development Strategy for the 1980s," *Economic and Political Weekly,* **21**: 845–852, 1984.

[9] Chenery, Hollis, and Michael Bruno "Development Alternatives in an Open Economy: The Case of Israel," *Economic Journal,* **72**: 79–103, 1962.

[10] Diaz-Alejandro, Carlos "A Note on the Impact of Devaluation and the Redistributive Effect," *Journal of Political Economy,* **71**: 577–80, 1963.

[11] Diaz-Alejandro, Carlos "Southern Cone Stabilization Plans," in William Cline and Sidney Weintraub (eds.) *Economic Stabilization in Developing Countries,* Brookings Institution, 1981.

[12] Dutt, Amitava "Stagnation, Income Distribution, and Monopoly Power," *Cambridge Journal of Economics,* **8**: 25–40, 1984.

[13] Franco, Gustavo "Aspects of the Economics of Hyperinflations: Issues and Historical Studies of Four European Hyperinflations of the 1920's," Department of Economics, Harvard University, Unpublished Ph.D. dissertation, 1986.

[14] Frenkel, Roberto "Mercado Financiero, Expectativas Cambiales, y Movimientos de Capital," *Trimestre Economico,* **50**: 2041–76, 1983.

[15] Furtado, Celso *Analise do "Modelo" brasilerio,* Civilizacao Brasileira, 1972.

[16] Galbraith, John Kenneth "Market Structure and Stabilization Policy," *Review of Economics and Statistics,* **31**: 50–53, 1957.

[17] Gibson, Bill, "A Structuralist Macromodel for Post-Revolutionary Nicaragua," *Cambridge Journal of Economics,* **9**: 347–369, 1985.

[18] Giovannini, Alberto "Saving and the Real Interest Rate in LDC's," *Journal of Development Economics,* **18**: 197–217, 1985.

[19] Hirschman, Albert "Devaluation and the Trade Balance: A Note,'; *Review of Economics and Statistics,* **31**: 50–53, 1949.

[20] Kaldor, Nicholas *Causes of the Slow Rate of Growth of the United Kingdom,* Cambridge University Press, 1966.

[21] Kalecki, Michal *Selected Essays on the Dynamics of the Capitalist Economy,* Cambridge University Press, 1971.

[22] Kalecki, Michal, *Essays on Developing Economics,* Harvester Press, 1976.

[23] Kindleberger, Charles *Manias, Panics, and Crashes*: *A History of Financial Crises,* Basic Books, 1978.

[24] Krueger, Anne "The Political Economy of the Rent-Seeking Society," *American Economic Review,* **64**: 291–303, 1974.

[25] Krueger, Anne, *Liberalization Attempts and Consequences,* National Bureau of Economic Research, 1978.

[26] Lopes, Francisco "Inflacao Inercial, Hiperinflacao e Disinflacao: Notas e Conjecturas," Departmento de Economia, Pontificia Universidade Catolica, Rio de Janeiro, 1984.

[27] Lustig, Nora "Underconsumption in Latin American Economic Thought: Some Considerations," *Review of Radical Political Economics,* **12**: 35–43, 1980.

[28] Marglin, Stephen A., and Amit Bhaduri "Distribution, Capacity Utilization, and Growth" Department of Economics, Harvard University, 1986.

[29] McCarthy, F. Desmond, Lance Taylor and Cyrus Talati, "Trade Patterns in Developing Countries, 1964–82" *Journal of Development Economics,* to appear.

[30] McKinnon, Ronald, *Money and Capital in Economic Development* Brookings Institution, 1973.

[31] Minsky, Hyman, *Can "It" Happen Again? Essays on Instability and Finance* M. E. Sharpe, 1982.

[32] Nayyar, Deepak, "Industrial Development in India: Some Reflections on Growth and Stagnation," *Economic and Political weekly,* **12**: 1265–1278, 1978.

[33] Noyola Vasquez, Juan F. "El Desarrollo Economico y la Inflacion en Mexico y Otros Paises Latinoamericanos," *Investigacion Economica,* **16**: 603–48, 1956.

[34] Ocampo, Jose Antonio, "The Macroeconomic Effect of Import Controls: A Keynesian Analysis," *Journal of Development Economics, to appear.*

[35] Sarkar, Hiren, and Manoj Panda, "Administered Prices, Inflation, and Growth: Some Results for Indian Economy," National Council of Applied Economic Research, New Delhi, 1986.

[36] Shaw, Edward, *Financial Deepening in Economic Development,* Oxford University Press, 1973.

[37] Streeten, Paul and Thomas Balogh, "A Reconsideration of Monetary Policy," *Bulletin of the Oxford University Institute of Statistics,* **19**: 331–339, 1957.

[38] Sylos-Labini, Paolo, *The Forces of Economic Growth and Decline,* MIT Press, 1984.

[39] Tavares, Maria de Conceicao, *Da Substituicao de Importacoes ao Capitalism Financieiro,* Zahar Editores, 1972.

[40] Taylor, Lance, *Structuralist Macoreconomics* Basic Books, 1983.

[41] Taylor, Lance, "*A Stagnationist Model of Economic Growth,*" *Cambridge Journal of Economics,* **9**: 383–403, 1985.

[42] Taylor, Lance, "Demand Composition, Income Distribution, and Growth," Department of Economics, Massachusetts Institute of Technology, 1985.

[43] Taylor, Lance, "Economic Openness: Problems to Century's End," Department of Economics, Massachusetts Institute of Technology, 1986.

[44] Taylor, Lance, *Varieties of Stabilization Experience: Toward Sensible Macroeconomics in the Third World,* Clarendon Press, 1988.

[45] Taylor, Lance and Edmar L. Bacha, "The Unequalizing Spiral: A First Growth Model for Belindia," *Quarterly Journal of Economics,* **90**: 197–218, 1976.

[46] Taylor, Lance and Susan Horton, "Food Subsidy Programs: Theory, Practice, and Policy Lessons," Department of Economics, Massachusetts Institute of Technology, 1986.

[47] Taylor, Lance and Stephen O'Connell, "A Minsky Crisis," *Quarterly Journal of Economics,* **100**: 871–85, 1988.

Appendix

Algebraic expressions underlying the diagrams presented in the text appear here. We begin with the 2×2 system for capacity utilization u and the trade surplus t in Eqs. (16) and (17). Let Ω stand for the absolute value of the negative term in brackets multiplying u in (16). Then the total differential of (16) and (17) is

$$\begin{bmatrix} -\Omega & q \\ -[P_0^* a + (1-\theta)P_i^* \beta h] & -1 \end{bmatrix} \begin{bmatrix} du \\ dt \end{bmatrix}$$

$$+ \begin{bmatrix} -\left[h(\theta + q(1-\theta)P_i^*) + \dfrac{s\omega u}{(1+\tau)(1+v)(1+i\omega)^2}\right] \\ (1-\theta)P_i^* h \end{bmatrix} di$$

$$+ \begin{bmatrix} c_0' + (\theta + q(1-\theta)P_i^*)h \\ -(1-\theta)P_i^* h \end{bmatrix} d\hat{P} + \begin{bmatrix} \dfrac{-u}{(1+v)^2} \\ 0 \end{bmatrix} dv + \begin{bmatrix} 1 \\ 0 \end{bmatrix} d\gamma \qquad \text{(A.1)}$$

$$+ \begin{bmatrix} (\Theta + (1-\theta)P_i^*)g_0' + \dfrac{u}{(1+v)(1+\tau)^2}\left(h - s + \dfrac{si\omega}{1+i\omega}\right) \\ -(1-\theta)P_i^* g_0' \end{bmatrix} d\tau$$

$$+ \begin{bmatrix} 0 \\ -(1-\theta)P_i^* hu \end{bmatrix} d\beta$$

$$+ \begin{bmatrix} \dfrac{(1-\zeta)\varepsilon}{q} - P_0^* au + \zeta\varepsilon_q \\ \dfrac{-(1-\zeta)\varepsilon}{q} + \dfrac{(1-\zeta)\varepsilon_q}{q} \end{bmatrix} dq + \begin{bmatrix} \varepsilon + \zeta\varepsilon_\zeta \\ \dfrac{-\varepsilon}{q} + \dfrac{1-\zeta}{q} \end{bmatrix} \delta\zeta = \begin{bmatrix} 0 \\ 0 \end{bmatrix}$$

where c_0' is the derivative of c_0 with respect to P, g_0' is the derivative of g_0 with respect to τ, and ε_q and ε_ζ are partial derivatives of ε.

The real exchange rate q and the real wage z depend on other variables in the system, as follows:

$$dq = \frac{q}{e}(1-\phi)de - \frac{q}{1+v}dv - \frac{q}{1+\tau}d\tau - \frac{q\omega}{1+i\omega}di - \frac{q}{w}(-\phi)\,dw \qquad \text{(A.2)}$$

and

$$dz = \frac{z}{w}\phi\, dw - \frac{z}{1+v}\, dv - \frac{z}{1+\tau}\, d\tau - \frac{z\omega}{1+i\omega}\, di - \frac{z}{e}\phi\, de \quad \text{(A.3)}$$

where ϕ is the share of intermediates in prime cost.

The differential of the scale factor β also enters the deliberations. It is

$$d\beta = \beta\left\{\frac{1+\theta^*\tau}{\tau(1+\tau)}\, d\tau - \frac{1-\theta^*}{1+v}\, dv - \frac{\theta^*}{e}(1-\phi)\, de + \frac{\theta^*\omega}{1+i\omega}\, di + \frac{\theta^*}{w}(1-\phi)\, dw\right\} \quad \text{(A.4)}$$

where

$$\theta^* = (1-\theta)qP_i^*/[\theta + (a-\theta)qP_i^*].$$

Inflation and the interest rate are determined by Eqs. (6) and (20). Note that neither variable is directly dependent on the trade surplus t, though they do depend on capacity utilization u. The total differentials of these equations are:

$$\begin{bmatrix} \delta_i & \delta_{\hat{P}} \\ \dfrac{(1-\phi)\lambda z\omega}{1+i\omega} & -1 \end{bmatrix}\begin{bmatrix} di \\ d\hat{P} \end{bmatrix} + \begin{bmatrix} \delta_u \\ \dfrac{\tau\alpha}{1+\tau} + (1-\phi) \end{bmatrix} du + \begin{bmatrix} 0 \\ \dfrac{(1-\phi)z\lambda\tau}{1+\tau} \end{bmatrix} d\tau/\tau + \begin{bmatrix} 0 \\ \dfrac{(1-\phi)\lambda zv}{1+v} \end{bmatrix} du/v$$
$$+ \begin{bmatrix} \dfrac{\delta(\delta-\mu)e\rho}{\mu(1+e\rho)} \\ (1-\rho)\lambda z\phi \end{bmatrix} de/e + \begin{bmatrix} 0 \\ -(1-\phi)\lambda z\phi \end{bmatrix} dw/w + \begin{bmatrix} 0 \\ \phi \end{bmatrix} d\hat{e}$$
$$+ \begin{bmatrix} \dfrac{\delta^2}{\mu(1+e\rho)} \\ 0 \end{bmatrix} dV + \begin{bmatrix} \dfrac{\delta(\delta-\mu)e}{\mu(1+e\rho)} \\ 0 \end{bmatrix} d\rho - \begin{bmatrix} \dfrac{\delta}{\mu} \\ 0 \end{bmatrix} d\mu = \begin{bmatrix} 0 \\ 0 \end{bmatrix} \quad \text{(A.5)}$$

in which (A.2) and (A.3) have been used to substitute out terms in dq and dz.

The sign pattern of the inverse of the Jacobean matrix for di and $d\hat{P}$ in (A.5) is

$$\begin{bmatrix} - & -\,- \\ - & -\,- \end{bmatrix}$$

where the duplicated signs indicate strong effects, i.e., fairly strong asset substitution in response to changes in the inflation rate ($\delta_{\hat{P}} \gg 0$) and a weak effect of the interest rate on inflation. Then both i and $\hat{P}$ unambiguously rise with τ and e, fall with w, and so on.

In asset markets, the total differentials of (38) and (39) are

$$\begin{bmatrix} W\delta_i & -W\delta_R R/RP_y^2 + \delta y \\ (W/P_y)\chi_i & -(W\chi_R R/P_Y^3 + \bar{W}\chi/P_y^2) \end{bmatrix} \begin{bmatrix} di \\ \overline{dP_y} \end{bmatrix} + \begin{bmatrix} w\delta_{\hat{P}} \\ (W/P_y)\chi_{\hat{P}} \end{bmatrix} d\hat{P} + \begin{bmatrix} (W/P_y)\delta_R \\ (W/P_y^2)\chi_R \end{bmatrix} dR$$

$$+ \begin{bmatrix} W\delta_u \\ (W/P_y)\chi_u \end{bmatrix} du + \begin{bmatrix} \delta P_y \\ -(1-\chi) \end{bmatrix} dy + \begin{bmatrix} -(1+e\rho) \\ 0 \end{bmatrix} d\mu = \begin{bmatrix} 0 \\ 0 \end{bmatrix} \quad \text{(A.6)}$$

Where $\bar{W} = V + e\rho + 1$ is the predetermined component of wealth (divided by government debt) in the short run.

INDEX

Kolibri 360 GmbH
Ferdinand-Jühlke-Straße 7
99095 Erfurt, Deutschland
produktsicherheit@kolibri360.de